THE RISE OF
Robert Millikan

Robert A. Millikan

THE RISE OF

Robert Millikan

PORTRAIT OF A LIFE IN AMERICAN SCIENCE

Robert H. Kargon

Cornell University Press

ITHACA AND LONDON

First published 1982 by Cornell University Press.
Published in the United Kingdom by Cornell University Press Ltd.,
Ely House, 37 Dover Street, London W1X 4HQ.

International Standard Book Number 0-8014-1459-8
Library of Congress Catalog Card Number 81-15204
Printed in the United States of America
Librarians: Library of Congress cataloging information
appears on the last page of the book.

For my parents, Inez and Ira,
AND FOR
Marcia, Jeremy, and Dina,
ALWAYS, FOREVER

Contents

	Preface	11
1	A Brief Introduction	15
2	The Making of a Scientist	22
3	The Scientist as Investigator	43
4	The Scientist in Action	82
5	The Scientist as Sage	122
6	Recessional	151
	Bibliographical Note	173
	Abbreviations	175
	Notes	177
	Index	197

Illustrations

Robert A. Millikan   frontispiece
Silas Millikan   24
Mary Jane Andrews Millikan   25
The only boy in D. D. Priaulx's algebra class   26
Millikan at Oberlin   27
The college graduate   29
Millikan at Columbia   33
Millikan in Germany   38
A youthful Millikan, 1895   40
Millikan at Chicago   45
The oil-drop experiment   64
Millikan's diagram of the oil-drop experiment   65
Robert and Greta, 1912   68
The photoelectric effect   69
Lieutenant Colonel Millikan and Max   88
A. A. Noyes, G. E. Hale, and R. A. Millikan   112
Millikan sends instruments aloft   137
Albert Einstein, Marie Curie, and Millikan, 1924   143
The sage   149
Millikan reminisces   168

Preface

> A man lives not only his personal life, as an individual, but also, consciously or unconsciously, the life of his epoch and of his contemporaries.
>
> —Thomas Mann

I do not consider myself to be Robert Millikan's biographer. This book is not a full record of Millikan's life or even of his scientific career. It is an essay, very selective, on themes that are illustrated and illuminated by Millikan's life in American science. It is, as well, a portrait of the development of a scientist. The book is intended for an audience wider than that of scientists and historians of science. Thomas Mann's words quoted above help to explain my choice of this mode of exposition. Despite its limitations, the biographical approach offers an unmatched advantage: it permits us to embody our historical abstractions. Through the biographical mode we are able to work out in detail the mechanisms of change.

Robert Millikan was among the most famous of American scientists; to the public of the 1920s, Millikan represented science. The first American-born physicist to win the Nobel Prize, Millikan was a leader in the application of scientific research to military problems during World War I and a guiding force in the rise of the California Institute of Technology to a preeminent place in American scientific education and research. His life is therefore peculiarly suited to illuminate and provide texture for the vast changes that have taken place in science during the twentieth century. In this extended essay, I employ the biographical mode to explore several important aspects of this theme. Millikan was successively a teacher, researcher, administrator, entrepreneur, and sage. By describing the novel roles that he assumed, I suggest how science grew in complexity and carved out an essential place for itself in our general culture. These themes can be traced in Millikan's choices with respect both to his scientific studies and to the direction he gave to the California Institute of Technology.

The title of the book suggests another story, an American success story—double-edged, touching, and universal. I want to provide a glimpse (for a glimpse is all the materials will allow) of the inner man, of his doubts and uncertainties even while he was at the apex of his fame. The evolution of Millikan's early research program and its relation to his prize-winning work have not been systematically described in earlier accounts, nor has the context of his work on cosmic rays. And in describing Millikan's decline as a front-line scientist I shall broach a subject too often taboo in the history of science.

I thank the National Science Foundation for its support of my research. Without this support the work could not have been accomplished. The Fellowships Division of the National Endowment for the Humanities enabled me to devote my full energies to the project for one year at a critical time. The American Council of Learned Societies graciously furnished a grant-in-aid to enable me to enlarge my perspective and work in archives far from the Millikan Papers. I am very grateful for its assistance and encouragement.

I also thank Arnold Thackray, editor of *Isis,* and the History of Science Society for permission to use the material from an article published in *Isis,* volume 68. My thanks go too to Russell McCormmach and The Johns Hopkins University Press for permission to use material previously published in *Historical Studies in the Physical Sciences,* volume 8.

I am grateful to Judith Goodstein, archivist at the California Institute of Technology, for permission to quote from unpublished materials and for much congenial assistance. Thanks also to Jeremy Kargon, who furnished the schema of the oil-drop experiment in Chapter 3, and to the California Institute of Technology, which provided all of the photographs.

ROBERT H. KARGON

Baltimore, Maryland

THE RISE OF

Robert Millikan

1

A Brief Introduction

What is this atom which contains the whole,
This miracle which needs adjuncts so strange,
This, which imagined God and is the soul,
The steady star persisting amid change?
                              —John Masefield

When Robert Millikan arrived in Stockholm in May 1924, he looked the part of an American recipient of the Nobel Prize for physics. Trim, fit, with flashes of dark hair among the distinguished gray, Millikan seemed to exude the dynamic self-assurance expected of the New World. He came as the representative of an America that now commanded the center of the world stage; he accepted his prize as the living symbol of an American scientific enterprise that had earned the world's respect.

The post–World War United States was confident of its wealth and power and sure of its destiny. Within its borders the twentieth century was widely perceived to be what Henry Luce would later call the "American century," and American science was an important part of it. The frontier was now closed, the "savages" were pacified, and new challenges were needed to test the mettle of the grandchildren of the pioneers. There was an economic world to conquer; science and technology together would help to pioneer this new frontier. Science and technology would convert this metaphorical wilderness into settled farms.

Millikan was a fortunate selection to embody these themes. Born in Morrison, Illinois, in 1868, he liked to refer to himself as the grandson of pioneers of good, clean-cut stock. He wanted always to believe he carried within himself their virtue, their devotion to duty, and their modest success. As they had reduced the unknown wilderness to settlement, he searched out the mysteries within matter and the mysteries of radiation from the deepest recesses of outer space. The cover of *Time* magazine for April 25, 1927, on which the Great Scientist intently peers into a microscope, depicts this new American myth. The caption reads: "Dr. Robert Andrews Millikan . . . detected the cosmic pulse."

After decades of rapid change, the United States of the 1920s had need of myths. It had emerged from World War I, in the words of Arthur D. Little, as "the first industrial nation of the world."[1] It claimed the highest standard of living the world had ever known. Its industries and farms were vigorously productive. The war had stimulated the growth of entire new industries and pointed the way toward new conceptions of industrial and business organization.[2] From a debtor nation America had suddenly become the world's creditor.

The honor for this unprecedented wealth and power was portioned out among many sources, but science and technology, heirs to the brash "know-how" of the Yankee, stood high on most lists. Secretary of Commerce Herbert Hoover, for example, saw the basis for prosperity in pure science:

> The more one observes, the more clearly does he see that it is in the soil of pure science that are found the origins of all our modern industry and commerce. In fact, our civilizations and our large populations are wholly built upon our scientific discoveries. It is the increased productivity of men which have come from these discoveries that has defeated the prophecies of Malthus.[3]

Robert Millikan, too, interpreted the past and predicted the future in this fashion. Armed with the pioneer heritage and pioneer values, America would work out its destiny in the twentieth century. "Why is it," Millikan asked, "that 'fifty years of Europe is better than a cycle of Cathay'? Is it not simply because in certain sections of the world, primarily those inhabited by the Nordic race, a certain set of ideas have got a start in men's minds, the ideas of progress and of responsibility?"[4] For

Millikan, the answer lay in both mind and spirit, in science fortified by religion:

> Science imbued with the spirit of service which is the essence of religion, and religion guided by the intelligence, the intellectual honesty, the objectiveness which is characteristic of the spirit of science, can between them, without a shadow of a doubt, in view of the rate at which discoveries are being brought about, transform this world in a generation.[5]

The breathless prose reinforces his message: science can transform the world—*now*. America was for Millikan, as for many Americans of his generation and class, the master of the future, a nation chosen to lead. Individualism, fortitude, and know-how would ensure that future; science and technology would actualize those virtues. The American scientific community, most Americans believed, promised to play a major role in the new world.

This pervasive belief in the potency of science and technology had emerged within Millikan's lifetime. Much had changed in the years between 1868 and 1924. In 1874, when Robert Millikan was six years old, the famous astronomer Simon Newcomb wrote that America was "a generation behind the age in nearly every branch of exact science," and he attributed this gap to a "single proposition, that the American public has no adequate appreciation of the superiority of original research to simple knowledge. It is too prone to look upon great intellectual efforts as mere *tours de force*, worthy of more admiration than the feats of the gymnast, but not half so amusing, and no more in need of public support."[6] It is true that science's institutional base in America was relatively weak in 1870. By 1875 only a handful of physics Ph.D.s had been trained in America; the first sustained research and training program was to be established at Johns Hopkins under Henry Rowland in the late 1870s. Specialized journals in the sciences were nonexistent until the last quarter of the nineteenth century. Professional organizations, such as the American Physical Society, were well in the future. The infrastructure of the scientific professions existed only in embryo.

As Simon Newcomb noted, technology was often lauded in America, but science was more often seen as too abstract—worthy of respect, perhaps, but not of support. Many people identified science with "theory"—a word that for them was a pejorative. "The American people," one observer wrote, "is intent on studying not the hieroglyphic monuments of ancient genius, but how best to subdue and till the soil of the boundless territories.... The youth of this country are learning the sciences, not as theories, but with reference to their application to the arts."[7]

America and American science, however, were on the threshold of sea-changes. Science was about to become increasingly important in American life, and the status of scientists would correspondingly rise. In the next half century America itself was transformed—economically, materially, and socially. With the aid of science and technology, embryonic new industries were introduced: electricity, the internal combustion engine, commercial food canning, indoor plumbing, refrigeration.[8] America was becoming industrialized, urbanized, and modernized.

Accompanying this great transformation in American life was the rise of what John Kenneth Galbraith calls (in the corporate context) the "technostructure" of modern society,[9] or what Robert Wiebe has identified as the "new middle class"—those segments of society that possess the systematic training and skills so necessary to a modern technological nation.[10]

The new middle class staked out its claims for status, wealth, and influence on the basis of its expertise and the presumed value of that expertise for the health and wealth of the social body. It is no wonder that "science" became "the basic word that every school of thought claimed and worshipped."[11] The science they extolled was no longer solely the body of God's laws and his universe; it was a tool, a method to be applied to all areas of human concern, and the technostructure wielded it effectively. By the time Millikan's career reached its height in the mid-1920s, the power of organized knowledge was clearly evident, as in this editorial in *The World's Work* of 1925:

> The ideas that control science and business and professional life, are, above all, applicable to public affairs.... The trained man is

indispensable in practically every field. Medicine, the law, engineering, business organization—everywhere the mind that concentrates on one department and masters it in all its details, is in demand.[12]

The cadres of this urbanizing and industrializing nation, the new middle class, began to fill the new institutions created to produce and apply the scientific and technical knowledge demanded by post–Civil War America: the professional societies and organizations, the large corporations, and the universities.

The transformation in higher education, from the college as the molder of Christian gentlemen to the university as trainer of a new elite for the nation's service, has been widely discussed.[13] The leaders of the universities—Charles William Eliot of Harvard, Daniel Coit Gilman of Hopkins, Andrew Dickson White of Cornell, William Rainey Harper of Chicago, Charles Richard Van Hise of Wisconsin, and others—had understood it. As early as 1869 the new president of the University of Minnesota, William Folwell, encapsulated the new views:

> What we demand, then, is, not rules, but principles; not mere tricks of art and sleight of hand, but science; science which explains and authenticates art; which makes men masters in their work, and not mere imitators and operatives.... We need to put a solider basis of science not only under technical arts and learned professions but under commerce, government, and social relations.... I think then we have discovered what is that informing spirit which is to give life to the limbs and elements of the University; which can fuse, cement and compact them into a harmonious organization. It is Science.[14]

If science was reconceptualized as expertise or method, institutionally it was increasingly understood as enterprise. As the twentieth century was born and grew older, the notion that science, and a fortiori scientists, could be produced virtually on demand became incorporated into the common discourse. Universities produced scientists; university and industrial laboratories brought forth a bounty of science and technology.

This redefined "science" in turn helped to shape America's conception of progress. The twentieth-century success of science conformed neatly with many Americans' visions of a golden future. Science and technology reinforced their desire for control over that future and seemed to promise they would have that control. What had hitherto been viewed as God's blessings—resources, climate, fertile land—were now thought to be subject to the powerful force of organized knowledge. The General Electric Company's slogan "Progress is our most important product" epitomizes many of the assumptions, both overt and unstated, that lie in the American background.

Millikan himself made the same case before the 1926 graduating class of the California Institute of Technology, an institution whose superiority he helped to mold:

> Is it not the most sublime, the most stimulating conception that has ever entered human thought, this conception of *progress*, this new idea absolutely unknown in ancient times, a progress of which we are a part, and in which we are ourselves consciously playing a role of supreme importance? A progress which...the man on the streets now partially understands and certainly believes in; for has he not, in his own lifetime, seen the most capricious, the most terrible phenomena of nature, the thunderbolts of Jove, become the willing slaves of all mankind so that six million workers in America alone are today supported directly or indirectly by the electrical industry?...The supreme question for all mankind is how it can best stimulate and accelerate the application of the scientific method to all departments of human life.[15]

During the 1920s, such a statement was well within the consensus view. It had not always been so. Robert Millikan was both a contributor to the triumph of that view and its product. His rise to prominence both shaped and reflected the almost universally acknowledged role of science as a force in modern life.

In a remarkably clear way, then, Millikan's own life exemplifies the complex changes that vast enterprise known as science had undergone during his years. Within his lifetime the institutional substructure that bears the enterprise was laid down, strengthened, and expanded. During his long career the firm expertise represented by the scientific method brought within its compass vast new areas of American life. The "scientification" of

America eventually touched production, distribution, communication, advertising, politics, the making of war, and the making of love. Robert Millikan's scientific life highlights part of that process.

Arthur Compton wrote of him, "It would be difficult to find a person whose life is more representative of the course of modern history than is that of Robert A. Millikan."[16] But in what way representative? Millikan's life in American science was a microcosm of new roles assumed by the scientist during the course of the twentieth century. As science became more fully integrated into national life, as it became itself a complex enterprise charged with the production of trained personnel, of services, and of products, the scientists who comprised the enterprise assumed new career patterns. The professionalization of science invoked the scientist as teacher, as researcher, as administrator and fund raiser, as consultant, and finally as celebrity and sage. Millikan filled all these roles. At Chicago he blossomed as teacher and researcher; he was a valued consultant for the American Telephone and Telegraph Company and for the United States Government; he served as de facto president of the California Institute of Technology; during the 1920s and 1930s his name was well known to readers of popular magazines and newspapers. In the words of a 1932 citation, he was "a prophet of the new time."[17]

2

The Making of a Scientist

> If you find your task is hard,
> Try, try again;
> Time will bring you your reward.
> Try, try again.
> —*McGuffey's Reader*

Maquoketa, Iowa, where Robert Millikan grew to manhood, lies in the rolling prairie country of Jackson County, rising gently from the river to high bluffs. The land is fertile and rich; Maquoketa's farmers harvest a bounty of corn, oats, and wheat. When Silas and Mary Jane Millikan arrived with their children in 1875, Robbie, their second-born, was seven. The town was already over a generation old and boasted about 2,500 inhabitants. The early settlers had been drawn to Maquoketa from New York, New England, Virginia, and Pennsylvania by the promise of good land and good weather. Enterprising merchants soon built substantial trading firms, and in their wake came schools, banks, and churches. Even in the nineteenth century most Maquoketans were regarded as belonging to the "best class"; they had "good taste" and "a reputation for probity in business."[1] Millikan remembered the town as having "more than its share of families of background, ideals and culture."[2]

The Congregational church, in which Silas Millikan came to preach, was the first in Maquoketa, built scarcely more than twenty years before his arrival. Congregationalism was then burgeoning in a rapidly growing Iowa. Between 1840 and 1880 Iowa's population rose from 43,000 to 1.625 million. Congregational churches multiplied from a mere 3 in 1838 to 234 in 1880, serving more than 15,500 members.[3]

The Congregationalists stressed a "settled ministry"; they liked to contrast their own ministers, who were often good scholars and capable preachers, with the less well-prepared ones of the Methodists.[4] Silas Millikan was certainly well prepared. He had earned degrees from both Oberlin College and the Oberlin Theological Seminary. His wife, the former Mary Jane Andrews, followed the evangelist Charles G. Finney from her home in Rochester, New York, to Oberlin. She, too, took her degree at Oberlin in 1857, and afterward served as dean of women at Olivet College in Michigan. Millikan remembered her as having an "exceedingly well-balanced mind, even tempered sound judgment and good literary taste."[5]

A puritan upbringing molded Robbie's character. Silas and Mary Jane raised their six children (Allen, Robert, Max, Grace, Marjorie, and Mabel) on a preacher's salary of $1,300 supplemented by the produce of their acre of land and milk from two cows. The children were expected to work hard to supplement the family income and to contribute to a savings account and to the church.[6] Millikan recalled his mother as a "thrifty" woman. She urged her sons to count on their father only for room and board; otherwise they were required to shift for themselves.[7]

How early young Millikan internalized the self-help ethos is revealed by a surviving letter from Robbie, age six, to his father, a cool and distant man:

> Dear Papa:
>   I love you. I hope you will have a happy year. I'll try to be a good boy to make you happy. I'll learn to read and work and sing. I want to earn money to buy food for the birds and for missionary Sunday.
>
> > Your little boy,
> > ROBBIE[8]

What we know about Millikan's childhood depends largely on what he chose to collect and recall for us in later years. This situation has its benefits as well as its disadvantages, for although Millikan screened his distant past, what he chose to

Silas Millikan. Courtesy of the Archives, California Institute of Technology.

Mary Jane Andrews Millikan. Courtesy of the Archives, California Institute of Technology.

recall or to save assumes special significance. He seemed to remember himself as "undersized," "not a leader," not as "rugged" as the others, but as a consequence "more persistent, ambitious and aggressive."[9] He regarded himself as a figure in an American success story: battling to overcome obstacles, young Robert strove to make himself into a winner. Life was a competition, every problem a test of character. In competition, however, the other side of the elation of winning is the fear of

The only boy in D. D. Priaulx's algebra class. Courtesy of the Archives, California Institute of Technology

losing. This uncertainty, this fear of not making the grade or failing to please, stayed with him all his life. Even during those years when he established a reputation for arrogance and self-willed confidence, he privately confessed self-doubt and fears. Late in his life he wrote to his son Max: "I think I myself was at least forty before I felt at all confident that I could run a reasonably successful race with other physicists."[10] His profession, like all others, was created in the crucible of competition. Even after the Nobel Prize, wealth, fame, and security all were his, doubts continued to nag at him. In 1928, when he was

Millikan at Oberlin. Courtesy of the Archives, California Institute of Technology.

27

sixty, he confided to his son Glenn, "Even now in nearly every new group of surroundings I get the old sense of inadequacy."[11]

How much sharper this sense must have been for young Robbie, age seven, beginning life as the second of six children and already owing a considerable debt of labor and love to family and church. But Robbie strove to please. He worked hard, saved money, was punctual, and was diligent in all things. His report card from Maquoketa High School in September 1886 was splendid: "Robert Millikan," it said, "gained an excellent standing for good deportment, faithful application to duty and exceptionally high grade of scholarship."[12]

After graduation from high school, Robert worked in a sawmill and as a court stenographer to earn college expenses. Then he was off to Oberlin College, the alma mater of both of his parents and eventually of all of his siblings as well. He began, in the academic year 1886–87, as a student in the Department of Preparatory Instruction. He studied Latin under Mary Regal and Greek under John Fisher Peck. Millikan later wrote, "I owe a greater debt of gratitude to him [Peck] than to any one outside of my own immediate family, for the direction my life has taken." It was Peck that asked Millikan to teach his first class in physics and advised him to prepare for a career in physics at Columbia.[13] In 1887 Millikan entered the classical course at Oberlin. As a freshman he took trigonometry, analytic geometry, and mechanics, as well as Latin and Greek. During his sophomore year his science courses included chemistry, botany, and physics, the last employing the book by William R. Anthony and Cyrus F. Brackett as a text.[14] Robert regarded this course, taught by the Reverend Charles Henry Churchill, as poor; he purchased Elroy M. Avery's *Elementary Physics* (an 1876 abridgement of Adolphe Ganot's popular textbook) and worked out numerous problems by himself. When he was invited in 1889 to teach a junior physics course for the Preparatory Department, he assigned Avery's text.[15]

By the time he took his A. B. degree, in 1891, Millikan had had some calculus, a smattering of biology, a little astronomy, but no further physics. He decided to remain at Oberlin as a tutor at a salary of $600 per year, so that he could take

The college graduate. Courtesy of the Archives, California
Institute of Technology.

Oberlin's new "Scientific Course" of instruction while he continued to teach his physics class. The new curriculum was
"intended to constitute a course of liberal education rather
than one devoted to technical or professional training," and the
study of Greek was encouraged because "so large a proportion
of our scientific terms are of Greek origin." But despite the
classical cast of the curriculum, Oberlin's natural science offerings were considerably expanded and improved. In the two
additional years he spent there, Robert took geology, analytical
mechanics (with Frederick Anderegg), mathematics, and Ger-

man. He also completed what is described as three courses in physics; they were probably additional mechanics courses designed for graduates by Anderegg and Edward Roe.[16] His master's thesis consisted of a close reading of the fourth edition of Sylvanus P. Thompson's *Dynamo-Electric Machinery*, which had first appeared in 1884.

At Oberlin, Millikan took time enough to find his way. Encouraged by Peck, he slowly, patiently forged ahead on his own path toward a career in physics. The feelings of insecurity that had plagued him reappeared, however, in more vigorous form: "I was terribly blue," he recalled years afterward, "because the other men whom I admired got their work so much more easily than I got mine."[17] When he was awarded a fellowship for graduate work in physics at Columbia University, he was surprised.

At that time Columbia's physics department was not among the most prestigious or productive departments. In the early 1890s, Americans who insisted on advanced training and a doctorate usually selected a German university or attended The Johns Hopkins University, which had pioneered advanced scientific training in the United States. Between 1890 and 1895 Hopkins easily outdistanced any American competitor, producing eleven Ph.D.s in physics. By comparison, Cornell graduated four, Harvard none, Princeton one, and Yale four. At least fourteen Americans received doctoral degrees in physics from German universities. Columbia, it appears, had yet to produce the first physicist from its Faculty of Pure Science.[18]

While no American university laboratory of the 1890s could compete on equal terms with that of Berlin or Cambridge, several did offer attractive possibilities. Johns Hopkins, under Henry Rowland, was easily the most exciting. Rowland had been brought to Hopkins in 1876 by its first president, Daniel Coit Gilman, as part of a broad effort to implement new conceptions of the American university. Gilman intended to make Hopkins a model for advanced teaching and research, and in physics, chemistry, biology, and mathematics he achieved remarkable early success. Whether one judges his graduates by quantity or by quality, Rowland was by far the leading research director in the United States.

Other alternatives for Millikan might perhaps have been the University of Chicago, which had just hired Albert A. Michelson as professor; Harvard, which had both John Trowbridge and Rowland's student Edwin H. Hall; Cornell, where Edward L. Nichols had just begun the *Physical Review* and was mounting an impressive effort to bring students to Ithaca; Clark University, where A. G. Webster had replaced Michelson; and Yale University, where Charles Hastings, J. Willard Gibbs, and the recently acquired instructor Henry A. Bumstead made New Haven a formidable center.

American graduate training programs generally placed great emphasis on rigorous experimental research. The advanced work of potential Ph.D.s often centered on precision measurement, sometimes by means of instruments designed by the research director. At Johns Hopkins, for example, most doctoral dissertations in the 1890s involved applications of Rowland's widely admired concave grating for spectroscopic work.

A respect for precision measurement conformed well to the evolving character of American higher education. The traditional American college had been the citadel of discipline and piety. Its aim was to mold and finish Christian gentlemen who would, upon completion of their studies, assume positions of leadership. The key concept that informed the college was mental discipline.[19] Students were to be trained to think in a rigorous manner, paying much attention to matters of detail and good form. Study of the classics and mathematics, as well as the enforcement of a strict personal code of conduct, were means to those ends. Noah Porter of Yale, a spokesman for the traditionalists, insisted that "to hold the student to minute fidelity in little things is an enforcement of one of the most significant maxims of the Gospel."[20]

Under the pressures of post–Civil War growth and change, higher education in the United States was reformed. The attractiveness of "mental discipline" remained, but the concept was newly defined; Gilman's insistence that the new Johns Hopkins University "will always be a place for the development of character" was not mere rhetoric.[21] The new definition of mental discipline would incorporate Hopkins' emphasis on systematic research as well as new ideas of the social role of the graduate.

For Henry Rowland, the burden of imparting mental discipline to the student had shifted from the classics and moral philosophy to the natural sciences: the modern world demanded an educated leadership of "doers." "The object of education," he wrote in 1886, "is not only to produce a man who *knows,* but one who *does;* who makes his mark in the struggle of life and succeeds well in whatever he undertakes: who can solve the problems of nature and of humanity as they arise, and who, when he knows he is right, can boldly convince the world of the fact. Men of action are needed as well as men of thought."

The mental and moral discipline demanded by the laboratory is ideal for the purpose. Direct confrontation with nature produces the pragmatic modern man:

> To produce men of action, they must be trained in action.... If they study the sciences, they must enter the laboratory and stand face to face with nature; they must learn to test their knowledge constantly and thus see for themselves the sad results of vague speculation; they must learn by direct experiment that their own mind is liable to error. They must try experiment after experiment and work problem after problem until they become men of action and not of theory.

The man of science/action advances science through research; the applications and benefits to humankind will necessarily follow. But the important result is the generation of a disciplined mind capable of addressing all human problems: "This is the mind which is destined to govern the world in the future and to solve problems pertaining to politics and humanity as well as to inanimate nature.... And this is the mind the physical laboratory is built to cultivate."[22]

The graduate research program in physics at Hopkins, as at other American universities, centered on cultivating trained men rather than on exhaustively exploring a world view. The rigor of precise measurement was therefore both a mental and a moral test. To a student with Millikan's Calvinist outlook, this viewpoint had special appeal.

The Hopkins approach to graduate education in physics was

by far the most influential in America. Not only did Rowland produce the lion's share of Ph.D.s in physics in the last quarter of the nineteenth century, but many of the other major training centers bore his mark. Cornell's Edward L. Nichols had studied with Rowland and had done postdoctoral work with him.

Millikan at Columbia. Courtesy of the Archives, California Institute of Technology.

Harvard's Edwin H. Hall had been one of Rowland's prized students at Hopkins, and John Trowbridge had close contact with the Hopkins group and lectured in Baltimore. Charles Hastings had spent years at Hopkins as Ph.D. student and associate before becoming professor of physics at Yale in 1884. Henry Bumstead, who became an instructor at Yale in 1893 and director of its physics laboratory in 1906, had attended Hopkins as an undergraduate. In short, Rowland impressed his mark on American physics not only by example, but more directly by training its next generation.

Columbia's physics department lacked the vigor Millikan might have found at Hopkins, Yale, or Cornell. It drew few graduate students and seemed pallid beside the more vigorous departments of electrical engineering and mechanics, under Michael Pupin and Robert S. Woodward. Ernest Rutherford commented only a few years later, "The present status of Columbia in physical science is miserable."[23] The "physical laboratory" occupied a floor in Hamilton Hall, and was used for graduate and undergraduate instruction and for advanced research. The professor of physics was Ogden Rood (1832–1902), whom Millikan later described as "a strange appearing old man with long stringy hair" who worked mainly on problems in physiological optics and photometry.[24] Rood had had a leisurely education in physics. After he was graduated from Princeton, in 1852, he studied at Yale, and then spent four years in Germany. There he divided his time between oil painting and physics in Berlin and Munich. Upon his return to the United States he assumed a professorship of chemistry at the short-lived University of Troy (New York). In 1863 he was appointed to the faculty of Columbia University.[25]

Rood's subordinate, Adjunct Professor William Hallock, was engaged in measuring the specific gravities of jade samples and in devising new methods for the photography of flames, among other problems. He had received his doctorate at Würzburg in 1881 and had been associated with the U.S. Geological Survey and the Smithsonian's observatory before joining the Columbia faculty in 1892.[26] The chief assistant in the laboratory was Holbrook Cushman, who directed instruction. Cushman, like Hallock, had studied under Friedrich Wilhelm Kohlrausch at Würzburg, but he had not taken a degree.[27]

Millikan later claimed that he had preferred other teachers to those available in the Department of Physics. He singled out for special mention Michael Pupin, who taught electromagnetism, and Robert Woodward, who taught advanced mechanics. But in the end it was Rood that suggested his research topic and directed his work.

Millikan lost his fellowship after the first year. We do not know whether this loss reflects badly on Millikan's performance or on the Department of Physics, but it rocked Robert's shaky self-esteem: "I never dreamed I could make myself into an honest-to-goodness physicist."[28] He decided to enroll for a summer at the Ryerson Laboratory at the University of Chicago, primarily in order to work with Albert Michelson, one of America's most famous physicists. Michelson was a warm friend of Rood, and doubtless Millikan had the benefit of a personal introduction.[29] He attended Michelson's lectures during the summer of 1894, and was assigned a room in the laboratory. He conferred with Michelson several times that summer and was not disappointed by his contact with the well-known physicist.

Michelson had won a splendid reputation for himself, mainly through his precise measurements (1878–90) of the velocity of light and through the famous Michelson-Morley experiment on aether drift, in which he used an instrument of his own devising, the interferometer.[30] His new fame led to a chair in physics at research-oriented Clark University and eventually, in 1892, to a professorship at the University of Chicago and the directorship of its Ryerson Laboratory. By this time Michelson's concern for precision work had led him to devote his time to metrology. When he determined the length of the international meter bar kept at Sèvres to be equal to 1,553,164.03 wavelengths of the red spectral line of cadmium, Michelson became the international apostle of precise measurement. "In recognition of the methods which [he had] discovered for insuring exactness in measurements, and also of the investigations in spectrology which [he had] carried out in connection therewith," he was awarded the Nobel Prize for physics in 1907.[31]

In Chicago, Millikan attended the university's convocation in June 1894, when Michelson presented an address "on the place of very refined measurement in the progress of physics."[32] It was indeed a paean to precision: "Unquestionably,...by such work, and such work alone, must we look for the steady onward march of science, by which alone truth is to be dug from its well and placed upon a foundation more solid and more enduring than the pyramids."[33]

Michelson's personal example stirred the young man. Millikan often recounted the striking effect the handsome, impeccably attired older man had on younger physicists. "Elegance of observational technique, elegance of analysis, elegance of presentation,—these were," he recalled, "the impressions made on all of us younger men who had a chance to see Michelson's experimental work and hear him present it."[34] Michelson was the physicist Millikan wanted to be: he combined the patience, hard work, durability, hand and brain teamwork, exactitude, and refinement that Robert had been brought up to admire. He found in the older man a standard of excellence that had meaning for his own aspirations: "Altogether I was much more impressed by Michelson than by anyone I had thus far met. I felt for the first time in the presence of one which [sic] understood thoroughly and fundamentally in his own right rather than through books."[35]

After a rewarding summer, Robert returned to New York for Columbia's fall term of 1894. Having lost his fellowship, he supported himself through the year by tutoring undergraduates. Rood suggested a research problem in optics to him, and Millikan dutifully went to work on it. The fruit of his research was published in the *Transactions of the New York Academy of Sciences* in April 1895, and later in the *Physical Review:* "A Study of the Polarization of the Light Emitted by Incandescent Solid and Liquid Surfaces."[36] The problem had been raised and dealt with over seventy years earlier by the French physicist François Arago.

In 1824 Arago had reported that not all of the light emitted by luminous bodies is natural, as was generally supposed, but that some rays, especially those that come obliquely from the surface, are polarized. He hypothesized that a considerable portion of the light from an incandescent body radiates not from the surface but rather from interior layers of its substance. It is this "internal" radiation that is polarized, and it becomes so by having been refracted at the surface. Rood set Millikan on an exhaustive study of the phenomenon and a critical test of Arago's hypothesis. For the execution of the work, Millikan obtained the use of molten gold and silver at the United States Assay Office in New York. Using experimental equipment similar to that devised by Auguste Cornu during the 1880s, Millikan concluded that *all* light from incandescent solids and liquids undergoes refraction. He surmised that most of the light comes from the surface of the metal—despite Arago—and that the polarization is caused by reflection and refraction of the light in a minute layer of air that borders that surface.

At Columbia Millikan attached himself to Michael Pupin, a Serbian-born, American-educated scientist who had studied in Germany with Hermann von Helmholtz and Gustav Robert Kirchhoff. He was about ten years older than Millikan, and Robert looked to him for counsel. Pupin encouraged Millikan to complete his apprenticeship as a physicist by a trip to Germany to study with the great Helmholtz. But Helmholtz died before Millikan was ready to make the trip, and the young man had to seek out others during his *Wanderjahre*. In May 1895, equipped with a $300 loan from Pupin (at 7 percent interest), Millikan booked first-class passage on the steamer *Rotterdam* for $50. When he arrived in Europe he bought a bicycle and set off on it for Jena. He spent two months there, brushing up his German language and attending lectures by Eduard Winkelmann and Felix Auerbach. Then, accompanied by a friend, he began a bicycle tour of the Continent, taking time out in Paris to attend lectures by the famous French theoretical physicist Henri Poincaré. In the fall he settled down to serious business in Berlin. He registered for work with Max Planck, later to introduce the quantum, and with Emil Warburg. He also attended a physics colloquium where he saw Heinrich Rubens and Walther Kaufmann, who were assistants in Warburg's laboratory.[37]

Up to this point Millikan was sampling Germany's offerings. He remained nowhere long enough for sustained work. He attended Planck's lectures for a few months, but it is unclear how much he profited from them, for they demanded mathematical sophistication that he appears to have lacked. Planck's regular lecture cycle extended over six semesters; Millikan

Millikan in Germany. Courtesy of the Archives, California Institute of Technology.

barely had a taste of it. But he was there in Germany when shattering events were taking place. One of the most exciting physical issues discussed in Berlin in 1895 was the nature of cathode rays (or radiation in an evacuated glass discharge tube), about which German and British physicists were engaged in heated controversy. The problem was essentially resolved in 1897 by J. J. Thomson's discovery at Cambridge of a subatomic particle, the electron. A second lively topic was Wilhelm Roentgen's amazing discovery at Würzburg. In late December 1895, and again in early January before the Physical Society in Berlin, Roentgen announced the discovery, in the course of his cathode ray research, of a new kind of highly penetrating radiation, *X Strahlen* or X rays, which could produce amazing photographs. Within a year Henri Becquerel discovered "uranium rays," or what later came to be known as "radioactivity"—evidence of the natural evolution or mutability of the elements. Millikan was a witness to the birth of modern physics.

Having been caught up in the excitement of these still incomprehensible discoveries, Millikan realized that the physics discipline was at the threshold of major changes, changes unthinkable a few years earlier. But it was as a spectator rather than as a participant that he saw them. In the spring of 1896 he left Berlin and enrolled in Walther Nernst's physical chemistry laboratory in Göttingen. There he settled down for some sustained work in a borderland area between chemistry and physics. He took additional courses—with Woldemar Voigt in thermodynamics and with Felix Klein in geometry—but more important, he began a research problem.

Millikan undoubtedly felt more comfortable with Nernst than in the supercharged atmosphere of Berlin. At that time Nernst was interested in the dielectric constant, ϵ, as a key to understanding the structure of matter. He developed new. electromagnetic means of measuring this constant, and put numerous students to work on such measurements.[38] They found that a formula developed by Rudolph Clausius and Ottaviano Mossotti, relating the constant in a relatively simple way to density, worked well. Mossotti had, in addition, *explained* the formula, employing a model consisting of discrete conducting spheres (representing molecules) in an insulating medium. Nernst directed Millikan to test the formula, using a medium constructed along the lines suggested by Mossotti's model. Millikan measured the constant in an emulsion of water globules in an organic medium composed of benzol and chloroform. He found the Clausius-Mossotti formula to hold. The paper was published, with Nernst's approval, in 1897.[39]

Millikan often told his friends that the paper he sent to Nernst had included a long theoretical part explaining the anomalous dispersion curve he had obtained for the change of

A youthful Millikan, 1895. Courtesy of the Archives, California Institute of Technology.

the constant with the frequency of the electromagnetic waves employed in the measurements. Nernst refused to sponsor this part of the work and returned it. When Millikan's paper was published, he discovered that the editor of the journal had taken the hint and developed and published a very elegant and complete theory. Robert felt outflanked, and worked no more along those lines.[40]

In the spring of 1896 Millikan received an offer of a position as instructor in physics at his alma mater, Oberlin. The post was to pay $1,000 for three quarters, or $1,200 including the summer quarter. Millikan accepted. But when Michelson wired him that summer of the availability of an assistantship at Chicago, he jumped at the opportunity, though the pay was considerably less. "I have decided as I have," he wrote to Chicago's president, William Rainey Harper, "because I want the opportunity to do research work."[41]

Millikan's return to the United States marked the end of his apprenticeship and the beginning of his career as a physicist. When he left America for Germany in May 1895, he left as a young man trained in nineteenth-century physical science and socialized into a scientific profession appropriate to the post–Civil War American college system. As we have seen, the physical laboratory was viewed in influential circles as an instrument for character building, for the creation of disciplined and virtuous men. After an education in the classics, with some attention to appropriate but not overly sophisticated mathematics and mechanics, his concerns centered on the traditional interests of the experimental laboratory; as James Clerk Maxwell put it: "In experimental researches, strictly so called, the ultimate object is to measure something which we have already seen—to obtain a numerical estimate of some magnitude."[42] Of all the scientific leaders Millikan admired, no one epitomized both the scientific and the personal virtues of the laboratory so well as Michelson. The American system of training, with its emphasis on precision measurement, called for instrumental ingenuity, patience, and diligence. It was a training appropriate to a worldview in which science was seen as constructing, in Michelson's words, "a foundation more solid and more enduring than the pyramids."[43] It was appropriate also to a code of personal virtue equally unshakable. and incorruptible. For Millikan, Michelson once again pointed the way. Of Michelson he later wrote: "His most outstanding characteristic was his extraordinary honesty, his abhorrence alike of careless, inexact, ambiguous statement, as well as of all deception and misstatement. His was a remarkably clean-cut mind,"[44] These were the values that the American system of physics education were meant to impart, and which were imparted successfully to Millikan.

Millikan's experience in Germany did not shake these values, but rather broadened them. In Berlin and Göttingen he was exposed to the fever of research and the thrilling uncertainty of shifting world views. In a sense, Millikan was the provincial transported to the metropolis. And as if that were not enough, he was brought from the periphery to the center precisely at the time when the magnificent nineteenth-century picture of the world was beginning to splinter before the eyes of the physicists who had perfected it. Strange new emanations (X rays, Becquerel rays), what later came to be understood as transformations of hitherto "immutable" elements (radioactivity), and the discovery of smaller parts of hitherto irreducible atoms were all demanding the attention of researchers. The placid world of physics at Oberlin and Columbia was gone forever. Even if Millikan witnessed these events more as a spectator than as a participant, his hopes for distinction in research were high when he arrived at the University of Chicago's Ryerson Laboratory for the fall semester in 1896.

3

The Scientist as Investigator

> Once or twice though you should fail,
>   Try, try again;
> If you would at last, prevail,
>   Try, try again.
>   —*McGuffey's Reader*

Once Millikan was on the scene, his enthusiasm for the life of research may have been somewhat dampened. He was assigned a very heavy teaching load and was expected to write what he would later describe as "greatly needed textbooks." "The situation of which I found myself a part required this," he recalled, "quite independently of any preferences I might have had."[1] He worked a twelve-hour day, divided about equally between teaching and research. In general, however, the Ryerson atmosphere was not conducive to independent research efforts by young assistants.

Michelson, director of the laboratory and head of the Department of Physics, was the only significant physicist in the department; and after F. L. O. Wadsworth moved to the Yerkes Observatory in 1896, he was the only member who was actively publishing in research journals. Despite his reputation as one of America's most distinguished scientists, his public posture was not designed to attract the brightest or the most ambitious young physicists to the department. At the dedication of the Ryerson Laboratory in 1894 he said:

> While it is never safe to affirm that the future of Physical Science has no marvels in store even more astonishing than those of the past, it seems probable that most of the grand underlying princi-

ples have been firmly established, and that further advances are to be sought chiefly in the rigorous applications of these principles to all the phenomena which come under our notice. It is here that the science of measurement shows its importance—where the quantitative results are more to be desired than qualitative work.... An eminent physicist has remarked that the future truths of Physical Science are to be looked for in the sixth place of decimals.*[2]

Such sentiments were not unusual before 1895.[3] What is astonishing is that they were published as the introductory remarks to the section devoted to the Physics Department in the University of Chicago's *Annual Register* for 1898–99—several years after the series of discoveries that rocked the world's physics communities. What is incredible is that the introduction was repeated unchanged in each year's *Register* until 1907, long after the advent of X rays, radioactivity, the electron, special relativity, and the introduction of the quantum. Michelson's reaction to the discovery of X rays reveals much about the atmosphere at the Ryerson: "I confess I do not see just how any important scientific or even practical application can be made of it.[4] Nevertheless, in 1896 he published two short and unmemorable papers on the subject, the first of which attempted to explain X rays on the basis of Lord Kelvin's discarded "ether-vortex theory," and suggested that they were probably "only cathode rays sifted by the various media they have traversed."[5] But these tentative steps were among the very few Michelson made into the murky waters of the new physics. Like other American institutions of the period, the Ryerson Laboratory under Michelson's direction acquired a reputation not for bold attack on frontier problems of physics, but for the precise

---

*Michelson's statement may be compared with a similarly worded one by James Clerk Maxwell. Maxwell's point, however, was strikingly different: "The opinion seems to have got abroad that in a few years all the great physical constants will have been approximately estimated, and that the only occupation which will then be left to men of science will be to carry on these measurements to another place of decimals. If this is really the state of things to which we are approaching, our Laboratory may perhaps become celebrated as a place of conscientious labour and consummate skill, but it will be out of place in the University." "Introductory Lecture on Experimental Physics," in *Scientific Papers of James Clerk Maxwell*, ed. W. D. Niven, 2 vols. (Cambridge, 1890), 2:244.

Millikan at Chicago. Courtesy of the Archives, California Institute of Technology.

measurement for which he was justly famed and for careful concern for undergraduate science education. The latter field was one in which the junior men of the 1890s—Samuel W. Stratton, Millikan, Charles Riborg Mann, and Henry Gordon Gale—worked diligently for many years. Thus the world of the Ryerson, into which Millikan would become socialized after 1896, was one that avoided the somewhat risky research programs of the new physics and remained committed to more traditional, safer endeavors.

On his arrival Millikan assumed responsibility for the freshman physics laboratory for the course taught by the associate professor in the department, Samuel Wesley Stratton (1861–1931). Stratton held a B.Sc. in mechanical engineering from the University of Illinois and taught mathematics, physics, and electrical engineering there before joining Chicago's new physics department in 1892. He oversaw the construction of the Ryerson and had the responsibility for developing apparatus for undergraduate instruction. He left Chicago in 1898 to become superintendent of U.S. Weights and Measures, the director of the National Bureau of Standards, and ultimately president of the Massachusetts Institute of Technology.

Charles Riborg Mann, like Millikan, was hired as an assistant at the Ryerson in the fall of 1896. Mann had been an undergraduate and graduate student in physics at Columbia, where he held a Tyndall fellowship from 1892 to 1895 while he completed his Ph.D. at Berlin. Mann very quickly turned to science and engineering education, a field he made his lifework after leaving Chicago in 1914.

The Ryerson's emphasis on physics pedagogy reflected pressures exerted by the university. President Harper intended Chicago to serve as a standard in the initiation of reforms that would result in the elevation and improvement of those high schools and colleges that funneled students into the university. Harper's plan, which he represented as "revolutionary,"[6] was to develop a system of formal alliances with small colleges and high schools. The purpose of these alliances was "the adjustment of educational activity, to the end that the standards of primary, secondary and collegiate training may be raised."[7] The affiliated work of the university was governed by an administrative board of which Harper was a member. Albion Small, the sociologist, was the board's director. Des Moines College, Kalamazoo College, Butler College, and Rush Medical College were among the associated colleges; the Morgan Park Academy of Chicago, Shimer Academy of Mount Carroll, the Kenwood Institute, the South Side Academy, and the Harvard School of Chicago were among the local preparatory schools integrated into the program. Under some of the arrangements, the university would pass on appointments, conduct examinations, and publish the academies' announcements in its official bulletins.[8]

The university was also eager to help the city of Chicago to raise its standards of primary and secondary education. Of the 5,000 teachers in Chicago public schools in 1898, less than 10 percent had received a college education.[9] The university, through the College for Teachers and the Pedagogical Department, wished to improve both that situation and the more general educational outlook. Harper noted in his report for 1898–99, in accordance with the ideas of John Dewey in *The School and Society*, that "if at one time there existed a sharp line between the work of higher education and that of the public schools, it is a matter for congratulation that this line has disappeared."[10] In later years Millikan recalled with some pride his summer classes for teachers and the testing out of his pedagogical ideas of local high school students.[11]

There were few graduate students in physics. Most of the graduate instruction was in the hands of Michelson, although Stratton offered a "research course" in the laboratory for graduate students, along with a course in experimental physics that was devoted chiefly to the repetition of classical experiments. Among the early graduate students were J. L. Lake, who never took his degree, and A. W. Whitney, who likewise did not finish, but who later taught mathematics and actuarial science at several universities and was associate general manager of the National Workmen's Compensation Service Bureau. The Ryerson's first two doctoral degrees were awarded to Isabelle Stone and Gordon F. Hull. Stone came to Chicago from Wellesley and took her Ph.D. in 1897; her dissertation, "On the Electrical Resistance of Thin Films," showed that the electrical resistance of thin silver films decreased with age.[12] After leaving Chicago she taught at the Bryn Mawr School, in Baltimore; at Vassar; and at Sweet Briar College. Hull, whose dissertation was titled "The Use of the Interferometer in the Study of Electrical Waves,"[13] eventually became professor of physics at Dartmouth.

The following year E. S. Johonnet received his doctorate for a thesis titled "The Thickness of the Black Spot in Liquid Films"[14] and left to teach at the Rose Polytechnic Institute. The best student in the department was Henry Gordon Gale, whose dissertation (1899) was titled "The Relation between the Index of Refraction and the Density of Air."[15] Gale was hired at once by the Ryerson as an assistant, and later rose to the rank of professor and chairman of the department.

Michelson was notorious for his lack of interest in working with graduate students. Millikan told the following story:

> I think it was in 1905 that he called me into his office and said, "If you can find some other way to handle it, I don't want to bother any more with this thesis business. What these graduate students do with my problems, if I turn them over to them, is either to spoil the problem for me because they haven't the capacity to handle it as I want it handled, and yet they make it impossible for me to discharge them and do the problem myself; or else, on the other hand, they get good results and at once begin to think the problem is theirs instead of mine.... So I prefer not to bother with graduate students' theses any more.[16]

Michelson had few students in any case, and not all of those turned out well.

Millikan began his career at Chicago handling the laboratory for Stratton's freshman course, and after Stratton left in 1898 he took over the entire course. He collaborated with Stratton on a textbook, *A College Course of Laboratory Experiments in General Physics* (1898),[17] and helped him with the advanced experimental physics course, in which there were three graduate students. By 1898 he also taught courses in heat, radiation, and electricity and magnetism.[18]

Millikan took on the protective coloration of the junior Ryerson physicist. He demonstrated diligence as a pedagogue and cautiously began his own research program. In collaboration with his colleagues he began to publish what were to become highly successful textbooks. In 1902 he published with C. R. Mann a translation of Paul Drude's very influential treatise on optics under the title *The Theory of Optics*. In the same year the first edition of his durable textbook *Mechanics, Molecular Physics, and Heat* appeared. In 1906 he teamed with Gale to publish *A Laboratory Course in Physics for Secondary Schools* and *A First Course in Physics*. Meanwhile he was making his way, rung by rung, up the academic ladder. In 1897 he was promoted to associate, in 1899 to instructor, and in 1902, the year of his marriage to Greta Blanchard, to assistant professor. He began to receive offers of new positions; he declined posts at Virginia in 1897 and at Oberlin once again in 1898.[19] In both cases, Michelson strongly urged him to stay. The desire to keep him may have been one reason that Michelson turned the weekly seminar increasingly over to Millikan.

Though he pushed forward without significant research publications, he knew that in the end his career would depend on his scientific attainments.[20] Research was, after all, the reason he had accepted the Chicago position with such alacrity. By his own testimony, Millikan devoted half of his twelve-hour workday to problems of research. His first effort was the publication of the results obtained in Nernst's laboratory; this paper appeared in *Annalen der Physik und Chemie* in February 1897. His next effort involved work growing out of his course in thermodynamics. In the report of the Ryerson Laboratory for 1898–99, he reported as work in progress the "experimental determination of the work done in the free expansion of gases."[21] Millikan began work on the problem late in 1897. "It was on the cooling of a gas by 'free expansion' by a novel technique—a modification of the so-called 'Clement and Desormes method'—through which I hoped to fix the ratio of the specific heats at constant pressure C_p and constant volume C_v...a theoretically very important relationship, more dependably than had been done by preceding experiments."[22] After over a year of diligent labor, the goal still eluded him, and he gave up this line of research and began to cast about for other projects.

In the history of science the reasons for research choices have always been elusive. Weighted with hindsight, the historian all too often accepts the pattern of a distinguished scientist's researches as "natural." As we approach the twentieth century, especially, the question of why a particular line of work is chosen dissolves; to most historians the answer seems obvious. The memoirs and autobiographies of leading figures have only increased the difficulties. Millikan's reminiscences, written between three and five decades later, are often misleading and sometimes incorrect. The student of Millikan's life and scientific career must reconstruct his mental set at moments critical for his work. The *Autobiography* systematically suppresses the verve and excitement of long-discarded but fruitful hypotheses, theories, and research programs in favor of a rather dull, linear, but successful choice of problem areas. Yet from the scraps of notes and jottings that Millikan has left us, and from the pattern of his published material, we may attempt to recreate his world view and test his memoirs.

Half a century later Millikan recalled that "about 1900 I went definitely into the field I had read upon rather carefully in Germany, namely, the broad field of 'the ionization of gases' or 'the conduction of electricity by ions,' a field of which radioactivity was a part."[23] In fact, the research area he describes was at the time one of the most exciting and potentially fruitful, and Millikan was well prepared to enter it. He had emerged from his training with Nernst with a particularly sensitive eye for problems of physical chemistry, and like Nernst, he was keenly interested in the use of electrical measurements. What Millikan called " 'the ionization of gases' or 'the conduction of electricity by ions' " was greatly stimulated by the work of J. J. Thomson and his students at the Cavendish Laboratory of the University of Cambridge. In February 1896 Thomson announced the discovery of an important property of X rays—that when they pass through a gas (or any other substance, as he then believed), they render it conductive, "even though the substance is in its normal state a perfect insulator." The process, he said, was "due to a kind of electrolysis"; that is, the substance is "turned into an electrolyte."[24] With Svante Arrhenius' theory of electrolytic dissociation at the cutting edge of the new physical chemistry advocated by Wilhelm Ostwald and Walther Nernst, problems of conductivity united the interests of physicists and chemists. With Thomson's discovery of the electron in 1897, powerful new questions emerged: what are the magnitude and nature of the charges on the ions (atoms charged by gain or loss of electrons) in gases and the nature of the process by which conductivity occurs?

In 1898 Thomson published a short book, *The Discharge of Electricity through Gases,* which was an expanded version of lectures given at Princeton in October 1896. The book serves superbly as an entrée into Millikan's physical world around 1900. Thomson wrote:

The close connection which exists between electrical and chemical phenomena—as shown, for example, in electrolysis—indicates that a knowledge of the relation between matter and electricity would lead not merely to an increase of our knowledge of electricity, but also of that of chemical action, and might indeed lead to an extension of the domain of electricity over that of chemistry. If we wish to study the relation between matter and electricity, the most promising course is to begin with the relation between electricity and matter in the gaseous state.[25]

While the world of chemicophysics was stimulated by these researches associated with ionization and dissociation, it received a tremendous boost from the work of Henri Becquerel and of Marie and Pierre Curie. Research on the "Becquerel rays" discovered in 1896 was facilitated by his discovery that, like X rays, radioactive substances have the property of rendering air conductive. Ernest Rutherford explained the process as ionization of the air.[26] The intensity of radioactivity could therefore be measured by the rate of discharge of an electroscope or by currents produced between condenser plates. With these electrical methods the Curies discovered radium in 1898.[27]

We know that Millikan's interest was turning in these directions before 1900. In a note on a flyleaf dated May 21, 1898, he specified as a research subject the "resistance of air in its relation to the velocity of the (falling) moving body," a problem he was to confront later in his electron work under other circumstances. But by the summer of 1899 he was making other kinds of queries. In a note dated July 30, 1899, he wrote: "I notice that a Holtz machine produced the second spark between distant knobs much easier than the first. Air is evidently ionized by first. Is not therefore discharge electrolytic?" Several months later he was still concerned with conductivity problems: "Can ionic and metallic conductivity," he wrote on September 17, "exist together in liquids?"[28]

In August 1900 Millikan had the splendid opportunity to attend the International Congress of Physics at Paris, which was mounted in connection with the Paris Universal Exposition of that year. He supervised an exhibit of Ryerson apparatus, which, according to the *Autobiography*, was awarded a "grand prix."[29] Millikan took the opportunity to attend lectures and demonstrations of radioactivity by Becquerel and the Curies. On his return he began work along two lines of research within the matrix of his new concerns: radioactivity and the electron theory of metals. By the summer of 1901 he listed among his "research subjects" the variation of contact electromotive force with temperature and the variation of the Peltier effect (the production of a current between two metals at different temperatures). These temperature-dependency studies grew from his increasing interest in problems related to the conductivity of metals. His first publication in the newer physics, however, grew out of work related to his deep interest in problems of radioactivity.

In April 1902 Robert married Greta Blanchard. After the couple's seven-month honeymoon in Europe, during which he had the opportunity to visit several laboratories, Millikan threw himself into his research. The emerging science of radioactivity drew together three exciting research fields: it bore on fundamental questions of the structure of matter, the character of radiation, and the relation of these questions to cosmology. He began to read widely in current radioactivity research and prepared lecture notes on the subject. His notes of October 1903 include discussions of cathode rays, the electron theory of matter, the theory of metallic conduction, Roentgen rays, and the recent work of Becquerel and the Curies.[30] His new research interests evolved symbiotically with his teaching. Whereas his lectures on molecular physics in 1900 drew heavily on P. G. Tait's *Properties of Matter,* published in 1885 and revised in 1899, and the *Popular Lectures* of Lord Kelvin, published in 1889, in 1904 he was lecturing on recent measurements of the charge of the electron, on recent advances in kinetic theory, and on radioactivity.[31]

Concern with the character and mechanisms of radioactive processes drew Millikan inexorably into the subatomic world. By the time he began his work, the evidence was already strong that radioactive phenomena consisted of changes in the nature of the atom itself, and that the energy required for such changes was a manifestation of subatomic energies. Becquerel and Marie Curie showed in their work on uranium and thorium that the activity of radioactive substances is proportional to the amount of radioactive element present and independent of its chemical form. Furthermore, radioactivity seemed to be independent of such physical conditions as pressure and temperature. "Radioactivity seems therefore to be as unalterable a property of matter as is weight itself," Millikan observed.[32] If he wanted to do research on the most basic of questions—the structure of matter—the subject of radioactivity was an obviously fruitful field to cultivate.

His excitement is evident in two popular articles he wrote early in 1904. The "dreams of the ancient alchemists are true," he wrote, "for the radioactive elements all appear to be slowly but spontaneously transmuting themselves into other elements."[33] A stunning success of the disintegration theory came when William Ramsay and Frederick Soddy, testing Rutherford's prediction that helium would be found to be one of the disintegration products of radioactive elements, "grew" helium in a radium preparation in July 1903: "They collected the emanation from fifty milligrams of radium bromide and, examining it in the spectroscope, found ... the characteristic lines of helium beginning to appear."[34]

Millikan was intrigued by this drama of atomic birth and death. The changes, he noted, were analogous to those that occurred among organic molecules. Complex organic structures were continually decaying into simpler ones and were setting free energies "put into them when the processes of life built them up into complex forms."[35] The pioneers of research in radioactivity had proved that some of the heaviest atoms tend to disintegrate into simpler ones. The organic analogy suggested to him "a profoundly interesting question": is there "any natural process which does, among the atoms, what the life process does among the molecules, i.e., which takes the simpler forms and builds them up again into more complex ones?"[36] This "profoundly interesting question" was one that reached far into his soul; he was to return to it decades later, when he believed he had found the answer in cosmic rays.

Following Marie Curie, he initiated a study of American radioactive ores in 1904 in order "to throw light upon the origin of radium and the other strongly radioactive ores."[37] In

March 1904, with the assistance of H. A. Nichols, assistant curator of geology at the Field Columbian Museum in Chicago, he set out to ascertain whether the radioactive substances found in pitchblende and other minerals were all decomposition products of uranium. To do so he had to determine the relation between the uranium content of the ores and their activity. He found that the relation was constant, and thus (he believed) supported the view that uranium was the parent of radium.[38] Interestingly, his Chicago colleague Herbert McCoy, of the Chemistry Department, undertook similar work at about the same time, and neither seems to have been aware of the work of the other. When Millikan later became aware of the more advanced work of others in the field, especially that of B. B. Boltwood and McCoy, his efforts along these lines ceased.[39]

Millikan continued, as well, his studies on electric discharges, in which he had shown a serious interest in 1899. He began a study of sparking potentials, a subject that at the moment yielded him nothing. There was a good deal of interest in the subject at Chicago: Robert F. Earhart's dissertation of 1900 (written under Michelson and Stratton) concerned the sparking potentials between plates at small distances.[40] Carl Kinsley, an instructor in 1902 and assistant professor in 1903, published "Short Spark Discharges" in the *Philosophical Magazine* in 1905,[41] and Millikan and his student George Moody Hobbs turned to the question about the same time. Hobbs's results were published in the *Philosophical Magazine* in 1905,[42] but Millikan reported that he "could not find what [he] was looking for, namely, a series of characteristic [electric] field strengths at which electrons began to be pulled out of the series of some ten different metals which I was using in the highest attainable vacuum."[43] From the work of Hobbs, who concluded "that the carriers of the discharge for small distances come from the metal and not from the gas"—that is, "the discharge is produced wholly or in part by the metal ions"[44]—and from Millikan's testimony, we may surmise that it was the electron theory of metals that provided the matrix for this work.

One of the subjects explored in Millikan's October 1903 notes on radioactivity was the theory of metallic conduction. Metallic behavior was an issue widely discussed in the first half decade of the twentieth century; many people believed that ordinary metals were radioactive,[45] and the theoretical understanding of the passage of electrons through metals was broached by the theories of conduction of Eduard Riecke, Paul Drude, J. J. Thomson, and H. A. Lorentz.

The first modern theory of "electrons" in metals had been proposed by Wilhelm Weber in the mid-nineteenth century. By the late 1890s his successors were attempting to forge a unified theory of metals, including both electromagnetic phenomena and such thermal-electric phenomena as Ohm's Law, and Seebeck effect, the Peltier effect, and the Thomson effect. They tried to include as well thermal conductivity, an extension suggested by the Wiedemann-Franz law of 1853, which held that at any given temperature the ratio of the thermal conductivity to the electrical conductivity is approximately the same for all metals.

The attempts of such German physicists as Eduard Riecke and Paul Drude and by such British physicists as J. J. Thomson to explain the electrical and thermal properties of metals by means of an electron theory rest on a model that perceives electrolytic conduction (electrolysis) and metallic conduction in the same way. Wilhelm Weber had suggested that metal molecules consisted of electrically charged particles moving with respect to one another, and that some would escape the molecule, move through the metal, and be "captured" by another molecule, only to continue on in the same fashion.[46] Eduard Riecke, Nernst's teacher, developed this model in an elaborate paper of 1898 entitled "Zur Theorie des Galvanismus und der Wärme" (On the Theory of Galvanism and Heat).[47] According to Riecke, both positive and negative electric particles move about in the space between the atoms of the metal. By assuming that the average velocity of the charges is approximately proportional to the absolute temperature, Riecke was able to develop relations between thermal and electrical conductivities, treatments of the Peltier and Thomson effects, and other thermoelectric relations. Paul Drude took up this model and applied to it the dynamical theory of heat. Drude assumed that the kinetic energy (energy of motion) of the moving charges was proportional to the average kinetic energy of a molecule of a perfect gas at the same temperature, and employing the elaborate mathematical structure of the dynamical theory of heat, he was able to arrive at formulas for thermal and electrical conductivity and those galvanic and thermal relations already discussed by Riecke.[48] In Drude's theory the electrons were of different kinds and sizes, although all were multiples of a single elementary charge.

In a paper presented for him at the Paris congress that Millikan attended, J. J. Thomson made an important change. According to his theory, a metal is a spongelike matrix of comparatively motionless positively charged particles, with small negative corpuscles or electrons moving through them at great speeds. In his book *The Conduction of Electricity through Gases,* published in 1903, Thomson applied this model to the much-discussed photoelectric effect. When light waves of sufficient frequency are permitted to illuminate certain metals, electrons are emitted from the surface. This phenomenon was eventually labeled the "photoelectric effect." Wilhelm Hallwachs had shown in 1888 that when ultraviolet light falls on a negatively charged zinc plate connected to an electroscope, the electroscope will discharge rapidly.[49] Philipp Lenard and J. J. Thomson independently demonstrated in 1899 that the discharge was caused by the emission of electrons from the metal.[50] After 1900 researchers expended considerable effort to establish the principal facts: metals may be arranged in a series of decreasing photoactivity, with rubidium and potassium heading the list; photoelectrons are emitted from a given metal only when light above a certain frequency is permitted to fall on it; and, strikingly, the maximum energy of the photoelectrons is independent of the *intensity* of the light and seems to depend only on *frequency*.[51] According to Thomson, "the photo-electric effect is due to the acquisition by the corpuscles [electrons] in the metal under the action of the ultraviolet light of sufficient kinetic energy to enable them to escape from the metal. The higher the temperature the greater would be the initial kinetic energy possessed by the corpuscles and the smaller the increment required to enable them to move fast enough to escape from the metal."[52] In short, Thomson's "dynamical gas" theory of metallic conduction suggests that the incoming light supplies enough kinetic energy to "boil" off electrons from the metal.

The photoelectric effect should therefore be greater at higher temperatures than at lower.

An alternative view had fundamentally different implications for the structure of matter. This view, developed by Lenard, pictured the emission of photoelectrons as caused by an atomic disintegration. Lenard argued that the energy for the emission of photoelectrons cannot be supplied by the incoming ultraviolet light, but must be possessed by the corpuscles before they are emitted. The light serves as a trigger that detonates an atomic disintegration or detachment of electric corpuscles, and consequently causes their emission.[53] Millikan designed an experiment to distinguish between Thomson's kinetic model and Lenard's trigger theory. If the latter was correct, he reasoned, it was to be expected that the rate of discharge and the kinetic energy of the electrons emitted would not be influenced by temperature, whereas in Thomson's theory the free electrons "boil" off with the help of the light, and therefore their energy *would* vary with temperature.[54]

Millikan then assigned George Winchester the problem of determining the effect of temperature on the photoelectric emission (a problem on which other researchers were actively engaged). Winchester's work formed the basis of his dissertation, submitted in 1907, and an article published in the *Physical Review* the same year.[55]

Millikan and Winchester made careful measurements of the rate of discharge and the velocity of projection electrons from a series of metals at temperatures ranging from 25° C to 125° C *in vacuo*. Ultraviolet light was passed through a hole onto metal electrodes connected to a negatively charged electrometer. They concluded that "the photoelectric effect *like radioactivity* is a phenomenon which is completely independent of temperature," and that "the escaping electrons are therefore not the free electrons of the metal, but are rather electrons which become detached from the atom because of the coincidence of their own natural periods with the periods of the impressed aether-waves."[56]

In pursuing their work on temperature dependence, Millikan and Winchester had been only two researchers in an ample field.[57] Moreover, Millikan's photoelectric work had not made the impact he had hoped for, and his work on what was later called "cold emission of metals"—the phenomenon of negatively charged metallic surfaces giving off current under large applied potentials—was for the moment fruitless. In his own eyes, his initial attempts to probe the fundamental problems of modern physics were failures. "So far," he remembered in his *Autobiography*, "I seemed to be having very little success as an experimental physicist."[58]

The close of his first decade at the University of Chicago, then, found Millikan dispirited. To be sure, he was a successful author of textbooks, was well regarded at the Ryerson and in the university, and had had several tempting offers of positions elsewhere. Yet his thirst for recognition as a researcher had gone unslaked. Although he had spent on research "every hour I could steal from my other pressing duties," he had produced little of major importance and certainly nothing that would qualify him for a "position of much distinction as a research physicist." He still wished desperately "to make good in a research career."[59] How, indeed, was a forty-year-old physicist to "make good" in modern physics?

At this point in his career, toward the end of 1907 and during most of 1908, he began the series of researches that led to his determination of the charge on the electron, researches that brought him his Nobel prize. But why? Why enter a crowded field and choose just this problem? Given our resources, a definitive answer is impossible. But a few informed speculations may be made. In the first place, despite his lack of satisfaction with his previous experimental forays into modern physics, he was insistent on research that would address itself to matters of central concern to advanced physical theory, that is, to research problems at what he and his professional colleagues perceived to be the frontier. He later recalled that "everyone was interested in the magnitude of the charge of the electron, for it is probably the most fundamental and invariable entity in the universe, though its value had never been measured up to this time with an accuracy even as good as a hundred per cent."[60] The charge on the electron, e, was a fundamental quantity for contemporary physical theory; without a precise knowledge of it, modern physics was a house built on sand.

Second, and perhaps equally basic to his decision, Millikan wanted to do work that would command the respect of Michelson and his Chicago colleagues, and earn the attention of the world's leading physicists as well. Michelson, it may be recalled, had insisted that "the grand underlying principles" of physics had been "firmly established," and that what was now required was precision—that is, rigorous application of these principles to all phenomena, or the physics of the sixth decimal place.[61] While such a program might not have appealed to some of the innovative young revolutionaries on the physics scene, it possessed a certain grandeur. It raised a standard of care, professionalism, and excellence that at the least could not be ignored by the physics community. Millikan's reaction to problem selection appears to have been complex. On the one hand, he was convinced by the events after 1895 that the foundations of physics were undergoing profound alteration; questions of atomic structure and evolution kindled his imagination. On the other hand, he retained profound respect for Michelson's canons of method and for his high standard of what both could agree was "good work." If Millikan was to "make good," he would conform to what he admired in Michelson: his exactness, his caution, his attempts to bring stability to a rapidly changing world of physics.

In a sense, then, Millikan's choice of the measurement of *e* as a research program reflects his decision to serve two masters. Such a measurement is a modern analogue of Michelson's precise determination of *c*, the speed of light. By such work Millikan would become the physicist of the sixth decimal place prophesied by Michelson, and at the same time would serve the basic needs of the new physics. His paper of 1910, "A New Modification of the Cloud Method of Determining the Elementary Electrical Charge and the Most Probable Value of That Charge," explained:

> Among all physical constants there are two which will be universally admitted to be of predominant importance; the one is the velocity of light, which now appears in many of the fundamental equations of theoretical physics, and the other is the ultimate, or elementary, electrical charge, a knowledge of which makes possible a determination of . . . a considerable number of other impor-

tant quantities. While the velocity of light is now known with a precision of one part in twenty thousands [Michelson's achievement], the value of the elementary electrical charge has...been exceedingly uncertain.[62]

The prehistory of Millikan's experiments in this area and the history of his successively more precise determinations of *e* have been treated elsewhere.[63] A brief review, however, will enable us to fix more clearly on the nature of his contributions.

Millikan had for a long time been carefully watching the work of J. J. Thomson and his students at the Cavendish Laboratory of Cambridge University. Thomson and others developed a method for measuring the charge on the electron known as the "cloud method." Another Cavendish researcher, C. T. R. Wilson, discovered that in supersaturated water vapor, charged atoms or ions can serve as condensation centers to form clouds of water droplets. In 1898 and 1899 Thomson employed Wilson's technique to ionize the air with X rays and perform measurements on the cloud that resulted. After determining the total charge on the cloud with an electrometer, Thomson indirectly measured the charge on an "average" drop.[64]

Another of Thomson's students, H. A. Wilson, improved and refined the cloud method. He began with a cloud of droplets formed between two metal plates. An electrical field of known strength was established between the plates, and could be switched off when necessary.

Using well-known theories, Wilson was able to deduce that when the field was switched off, the droplets of the cloud would fall by their own weight at a characteristic speed proportional to weight. When the field was switched on, their speed would be increased owing to the additional pull of the electric field. Wilson measured the rates of fall of the droplets at the sharp upper surface of the cloud, compared the "field-on" and "field-off" results, and calculated the average weight of the drops by a relationship known as Stokes' Law, which relates the velocity of descent of a small sphere through a fluid, its radius, its density, and the viscosity of the fluid.[65] Since the additional pull of the electrical field on the drops was proportional to the charge of the drops, he developed a relation for the charge, *e;*

$$e = 3.1 \times 10^{-9} \tfrac{g}{E} (V_x - V_g) V_g^{1/2}$$

where g is a known constant, E is the known field strength, and V_x and V_g are the measured speeds with field and without field, respectively. In Wilson's words, the measurements of V_x and V_g are "sufficient to determine *e* absolutely."[66] The advantages of Wilson's method over Thomson's were clear: It was not necessary to estimate either the number of drops in the cloud or the number of ions or to assume that each drop contained only one ion, for he made his measurements on those droplets whose rate of fall indicated that they had the smallest charges.[67]

The method had some serious shortcomings, however. The measurements of the terminal velocities V_x and V_g were made not on the same cloud, but on successive expansions of the chamber. The calculations, however, assume that the sizes of the droplets during all expansions are identical. In other words, the calculations were made as if the measurements were performed on the same cloud, whereas actually they were not. As Millikan noted, cloud conditions are very difficult to duplicate in successive expansions.[68] Wilson himself pointed to other difficulties: "Since the cloud begins to evaporate soon after it is formed, it is very important to get the measurement of its rate of fall over as quickly as possible." Moreover, the applied field strength was limited by the size of the available battery: "It would of course have been more satisfactory if observations could have been made...through a larger range of [potential differences] but to accomplish this with the battery available was not possible."[69]

Wilson made eleven sets of determinations of *e*, varying from 2.0×10^{-10} to 3.8×10^{-10} electrostatic units (e.s.u.), with a mean of 3.1×10^{-10}. This lack of consistency among the measurements and the experimental uncertainties involved in their determination, not all of which had been pointed out by Wilson, seemed to Millikan to provide a clear opportunity. Thomson and other research leaders acknowledged the fundamental importance of exact measurements of electronic charge,[70] and by Michelson's standards, existing measurements were imprecise and unsatisfactory.

In the fall of 1907 Millikan's dissatisfaction prompted him to retry Wilson's experiments. With his student Louis Begeman, he began, like Wilson, to employ X rays to ionize the clouds; they found, however, that the X-ray source was far too variable, leading to the marked differences in velocities that Wilson had noted in succeeding trials. Millikan and Begeman substituted 200 milligrams of a 1 percent radium compound for X rays as the ionizing source. They also followed Wilson's suggestion that a wider range of field strengths would improve the measurements; Millikan and Begeman's potential differences ranged from 1,600 to 3,000 volts. The results of ten sets of measurements netted a mean of 4.03×10^{-10} e.s.u. for e.[71]

Millikan continued to be troubled by difficulties in Wilson's method. Distortion, evaporation, and dissipation of the cloud made measurement possible only with great difficulty. Starting in the summer of 1908 he managed to turn the *problem* of dissipation of the cloud when the field was thrown on into an *advantage*.[72] He found that at sufficient field strength the dissipation of the cloud left individual droplets in view. If it was possible to make measurements on individual droplets, he believed, it would be possible to examine the effects of individual electrons, avoiding the uncertainties in Wilson's approach. He fixed on the so-called balanced-droplet method. He examined droplets in an electrical field, opposing the fall due to weight by a contrary electrical force just strong enough to keep the drop in "balance," or nearly so. Those droplets that remained suspended were the ones that had the proper weight to counter the upward pull of the electrical field. When the field was suddenly switched off, some of the drops would move downward slowly and others more rapidly. Millikan reasoned that the slow descenders (the lightest in weight) were those that also required the least charge to keep them balanced, and the rapidly falling ones were those with higher amounts of charge. He then measured the rate of fall. Using simple geometric considerations and Stokes' Law, Millikan was able to derive an expression for the total electrical charge on a drop with respect to the measured rate of fall.[73]

The problem remained to determine the unitary charge e from the total charge on the droplet, which, after all, might contain multiple charges. Millikan noted that all of the measured values were multiples of a single quantity, which he took to be the electron charge and which he fixed at 4.65×10^{-10} electrostatic units.[74]

Still troubled by evaporation from the droplets, Millikan fixed on a way to reduce it: instead of using water or alcohol as a medium, he used oil—a specially cleaned gas-engine oil and a slightly less dense machine oil.[75] Millikan commented many times on the origins of his flash of insight—his decision to turn to less volatile media. The most famous account is repeated in his *Autobiography*. He had attended a meeting of the British Association for the Advancement of Science in Winnipeg at the end of August 1909, and presented his paper on the measurement of e by the balanced-drop method. On the long return trip by train the idea gripped him:

> Riding back to Chicago from this meeting I looked out the window of the day coach at the Manitoba plains and suddenly said to myself, "What a fool I have been to try in this crude way to eliminate the vaporation of water droplets when mankind has spent the last three hundred years in improving clock oils for the very purpose of obtaining a lubricant that will scarcely evaporate at all."[76]

Whether this "Eureka" incident occurred at all may disappear forever into the folds of time and legend. Some clues to the evolution of the oil-drop idea may, however, be found in the published papers of 1910 and 1911. There Millikan gives full credit to J. Y. Lee for the invention of the "atomizer method" used in his experiments:

> The atomizer method of producing very minute but accurately spherical drops for the purpose of studying their behavior in fluid media, was first conceived and successfully carried out in January, 1908, at the Ryerson by Mr. J. Y. Lee, while he was engaged in a quantitative investigation of Brownian movements. His spheres were blown from Wood's metal, wax and other like substances which solidify at ordinary temperatures. Since then the method has been almost continuously in use here, upon this and a number of other problems, and elsewhere upon similar problems.[77]

In Chicago Millikan told Michelson that he had a way to measure the charge on the electron to an accuracy of one part in a thousand, "or else," he added somewhat dramatically, "I am no good."[78] Once again, Millikan turned his researches into a test of himself; the measurement of electron charge was to gauge his mettle.

In his new set of experiments, he was assisted by his student Harvey Fletcher. An atomizer was used to produce a fine cloud of drops of oil. The drops were permitted to fall between plates with known electric field strength. A telescope was mounted so that one might observe the drops as they floated down under the influence of gravity. When the electric field was switched off, the velocity of a drop under the influence of gravity (V_g)

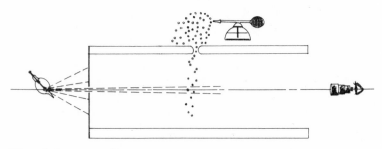

The oil-drop experiment.

was measured to yield information concerning the droplet's radius. When the field was switched on, the velocity under the influence of both gravity and retarding field (V_x) was measured. By careful observation of individual drops Millikan was able to measure *changes* in that velocity as the droplet gained or lost charge by capture or loss of an ion.

He easily derived an expression for the change in total charge on the drop in terms of the change in the drop's velocity.[79] Since a change in charge is reflected by a change in velocity, Millikan was able to "see" electrons jumping on and off his droplets, and in a sense measure the effect directly.[80]

He was able further to show that all of his changes in total electrical charge on a droplet were multiples of a quantity e, which he took to be the elementary charge on the electron.

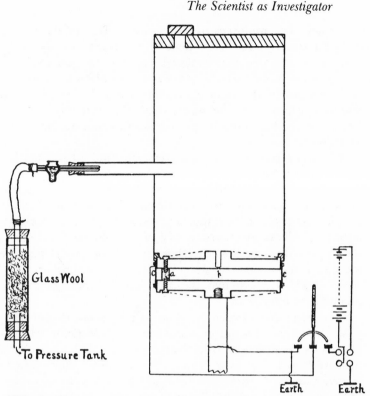

Millikan's diagram of the oil-drop experiment. From *Physical Review* 32 (1911):352.

From 1910 to 1917 his determinations for *e* were successively more refined:[81]

$$1910: e = 4.891 \times 10^{-10} \text{ e.s.u.}$$
$$1913: e = 4.774 \ (\pm \ 0.009) \times 10^{-10} \text{ e.s.u.}$$
$$1917: e = 4.774 \ (\pm \ 0.005) \times 10^{-10} \text{ e.s.u.}$$

What was striking to Millikan was his *direct* proof of the atomicity of electronic charge. While he had never doubted that there was an indivisible quantum of charge, Felix Ehrenhaft and others mounted a serious challenge to that view.[82] "Here then," Millikan insisted, "is direct unimpeachable proof that the electron is not a 'statistical mean' but rather the electrical charges found on ions all have either exactly the same value or else small exact multiples of that value."[83] His results showed that "the electron itself...is neither an uncertainty nor a hypothesis. It is a new experimental fact that this generation in which we live has for the first time seen." In Millikan's eyes, the measurement of the electron charge was to be his legacy to posterity, a legacy that he subsequently jealously guarded. He viewed it as his monument, which was not to be easily overturned.[84]

Millikan's electron work—an attempt to find a fixed marker among the shifting sands of modern physics—served his dual program by being significant to the physics of the subatomic world and precise enough to win the approval of such physicists as Michelson. His next important research effort, a thorough testing of Albert Einstein's theory of the photoelectric effect, was undertaken to restrain the excesses of modernity: he sought to brake what he was to call Einstein's "unthinkable," "bold," and "reckless" hypothesis of "an electromagnetic light corpuscle of energy hv."[85]

Millikan placed himself, at first, in opposition to Einstein's views; his research program was an essay in refutation. He saw himself as the defender of the wave theory of light: "To throw this overboard," he later wrote, "without even attempting to incorporate it into some new form of theory was clearly impossible, particularly in the Ryerson laboratory where we were working as continuously and familiarly with wavelengths as with meter sticks and where wavelengths were then—and still are now—just as real as foot-rules and spring balances."[86] There seemed no way to reconcile Einstein's photon with the truths of classical wave optics; to Millikan, intereference phenomena seemed to be intractable.

His earlier photoelectric work had been performed without reference to Einstein's theory. After his research with George Winchester on the temperature independence of the photoelectric effect, he tried to determine how the energy of the ejected electrons depended on the wavelength of the incoming light. His work "ran into snags."[87] He turned his attention during 1908 primarily to the electron measurements, but he continued his interest in photoelectric experiments, and in a paper presented to the Physical Society in December 1909 he reported a wider range of positive potentials assumed by metals under the influence of ultraviolet light than had hitherto been noted.[88] In 1911 he expanded on this work before the same society, reporting the production of "high speed electrons" with light from spark sources. He concluded that either the velocity of emission electrons is not independent of intensity (spark sources have a much higher intensity than mercury arc lamp sources) or that light possesses some quality apart from wavelength and intensity which is responsible for these differences. He noted that if the former is true, "one of the strongest arguments for a 'light-unit' is removed. In any case these results are completely at variance with the Planck-Einstein light-unit theory."[89] Within a year, further experiments forced him to recant his position that arc and spark light sources possessed different photoelectric properties; in fact they were the same, and his first blow against Einstein left its target unscathed.[90]

During the spring and summer of 1912 Millikan took leave from Chicago and went with his family to Europe. His expressed purpose was to find uninterrupted time to work up the further data he had collected on the electron charge. Making their way toward Germany, the Millikans visited Rutherford in Manchester and Sir William Ramsay in London. In Berlin the family rented a small apartment, and Millikan attended Max Planck's lectures on heat radiation. Planck "rejected as completely untenable the idea that radiation itself could be corpuscular (photonic) in nature."[91] Millikan also attended the weekly colloquia. At the German Physical Society meetings in July 1912 he reported on his oil-drop experiment and its results, and later in the summer he discussed his photoelectric work with the German physicists. The year 1912 witnessed an explosion of interest in the problem of the relationship between the kinetic energy of the photoelectrons and the frequency of the incoming light. There was considerable uncertainty about the relationship. In 1905 Einstein had maintained that light of frequency v communicates to the electrons an energy hv (h is Planck's constant), part of which is used up by the work spent in liberating the electron (ϕ) while the rest becomes kinetic energy T:

$$T = hv - \phi$$

Robert and Greta, 1912. Courtesy of the Archives, California Institute of Technology.

The German physicist Rudolf Ladenburg had insisted in 1907 that the kinetic energy was proportional to the *square* of the frequency. This view was developed by Jakob Kunz in 1909 and supported experimentally by David Cornelius of Illinois in

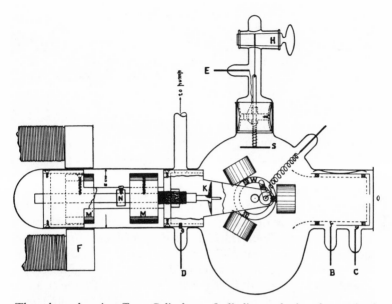

The photoelectric effect. Cylinders of alkali metal placed on wheel, *W*, kept clean by knife, *K*, operated by electromagnet, *F.* A beam of light, let in at *O*, falls on the surface. From *Physical Review* 7 (1916):362.

1913.[92] In a series of experimental and theoretical papers, O. W. Richardson, by himself and with K. T. Compton, proposed and buttressed a theory of photoelectricity that supported the *form* of Einstein's equation without assenting to his notion of the discrete (corpuscular or photonic) character of electromagnetic radiation.[93] A. L. Hughes supported the linearity of kinetic energy with frequency, but without mentioning Einstein, in an important paper of 1912.[94] By midsummer the German scientific community had become concerned with the topic, and such experimentalists as Robert Pohl and Peter Pringsheim were actively engaged in photoelectric work and were highly critical of existing measurements.[95] Millikan could not have left Berlin without increased concern for a topic that had engaged his interest for so long, the more so since Pohl and Pringsheim were preparing to publish a critique of Millikan's results concerning spark and arc sources in imparting speed to photoelectrons.[96]

On his return to Chicago Millikan hurriedly corrected his earlier photoelectric work[97] and began a new research program, a test of the Einstein-Richardson relationship, with an eye perhaps toward upsetting the applecart of those few who accepted the notion of the corpuscularity of light. Millikan suggested to his student William Kadesch that he undertake a more reliable measurement study of the energy of photoelectrons as a function of the frequency of incident light using sodium and potassium. In the published report of his thesis, Kadesch noted that "the total lack of agreement in experimental results, and the bearing of photo-electric phenomena on the unitary theories of radiation render it important that further work be done."[98] Since A. L. Hughes had discounted Millikan's results, and those of others who had measured photoelectron velocities, on the grounds that in their experiments surface film had retarded the electrons,[99] Kadesch used an ingenious device developed to clean the surfaces of the metals. He employed an auger-like knife rotated by an external magnet; the knife cleaned the metal surface *in vacuo.*[100] This arrangement was similar to the "vacuum workshop" employed later by Millikan. In any case, Kadesch's measurements argued capably for the linear relationship between frequency and kinetic enegy.

Millikan's first publication in the new program came in July 1914: "A Direct Determination of 'h,'" a short note in the *Physical Review.* Millikan's aims were broader than Kadesch's; he wanted to subject "to rigorous experimental test" three assertions contained in Einstein's photoelectric equation. He reexamined the linear relationship posited by Einstein between the frequency of the impressed light and the maximum energy of emission of electrons. He measured the slope of this line, which when multiplied by e yields Planck's constant h, and he also studied the assertion that the intercept on the frequency axis yields information concerning the frequency at which the metal becomes photoelectrically active. For his tests Millikan constructed an apparatus similar in concept to that of previous investigators but far more elaborate. A small block of alkali metal was illuminated in a very high vacuum, and the surface of the block was scraped by a cutter worked by an external magnet in order to keep the surface free of oxide film. The

photoelectrons emitted from the block were collected by copper oxide gauze connected to an electrometer. When Millikan
plotted the potential difference against frequency, his results
confirmed the Einstein equation. Using his own value for e, he
determined h "more sharply, more exactly and more certainly
than in connection with any other type of measurements thus
far made."[101] A fuller account of these researches appeared in
1916 as "A Direct Photoelectric Determination of 'h,'" again in
the *Physical Review*.[102]

Millikan continued his close examination of the Einstein
equation, publishing his results in several other articles that
appeared in 1916. "Although I have at times thought I had
evidence which was irreconcilable with that equation," he wrote,
"the longer I have worked and the more completely I have
eliminated sources of error the better has the equation been
found to predict the observed results."[103] Still, he insisted that
"the physical theory which gave rise to it seems to me to be
wholly untenable."[104] In his most elaborate treatment of the
problem, which presented a value for h precise to 0.5 percent,
he continued to attack the physical basis for the equation:
"Despite then the apparently complete success of the Einstein
equation, the physical theory of which it was designed to be the
symbolic expression is found so untenable that Einstein himself, I believe, no longer holds it."[105] He proposed instead what
he saw as a modification of Planck's formulation for black-body
radiation. According to Millikan, a given substance possesses a
large number of oscillators of a characteristic frequency or
frequencies, and a much smaller number of oscillators of every
conceivable frequency. If light of a particular frequency falls on
the substance,

> ... the oscillators in it which are in tune with the impressed waves
> may be assumed to absorb the incident waves until the energy
> content has reached a critical value when an explosion occurs and
> a corpuscle is shot out with an energy $h\nu$.... The emitted corpuscle
> never leaves the metal unless its energy of emission from the atom
> is greater than $h\nu$ but it takes place especially copiously when the
> impressed frequency coincides with a "natural frequency." ... This
> is little more than Planck's theory with the possibility of a corpus-
> cle being emitted from an atom with an energy greater than $h\nu$

eliminated for the sake of reconciling it with the experimental facts.[106]

Millikan's resonance theory avoids what for him was the "reckless" notion of localized energy and discontinuous absorption. As he wrote in a book published the following year (1917),

> We are in the position of having built a very perfect structure and then knocked out entirely the underpinning without causing the building to fall. It stands complete and apparently well tested, but without any visible means of support. These supports must obviously exist, and the most fascinating problem of modern physics is to find them. Experiment has outrun theory, or, better, guided by erroneous theory, it has discovered relationships which seem to be of the greatest interest and importance but the reasons for them are as yet not at all understood.[107]

Roger Stuewer, the historian of science, has justly called "shocking" Millikan's recollection in his *Autobiography* that his work seemed to him at the time to confirm Einstein's photon theory.[108] On the contrary, Millikan (like many others) still refused to concede the quantum character of light, although he did, in fact, see his work as supporting the views of Planck:

> The photo-electric results herewith presented constitute the best evidence thus far found for the correctness of the fundamental assumption of quantum theory, namely the discontinuous or explosive emission of energy by electronic oscillators. They furnish the most direct and most tangible evidence which we yet have for the actual physical reality of Planck's h.[109]

Millikan received the 1923 Nobel Prize for physics for "his work on the elementary charge of electricity and on the photoelectric effect."[110] The two research programs not only overlapped in time but also displayed similar general characteristics. In both cases Millikan demonstrated superb technical ingenuity rather than creative genius. He was gifted at entering an established research tradition and drawing the best results from it. In his electron work, for example, the basic problem situation had been laid out by J. Townsend, J. J. Thomson, and H. A. Wilson; the shift from cloud to droplet turned out to be critical, but even Millikan's most generous admirers will not claim it to be a flash of genius. In his photoelectric work he continued a path broken by O. W. Richardson, Karl Compton, and others.[111] Millikan's forte was his meticulous ability to eliminate error, often through clever modifications of existing apparatus. Paul Epstein, his colleague at the California Institute of Technology for many years, gave a perceptive account of Millikan's most common approach to research:

> He begins with a thorough study of the work of his predecessors, analyzing their methods with a view of discovering the weak points that could be improved upon. This enables him to start work with an experimental set-up eliminating some of the previous sources of error. Since the problems treated by Millikan are among the most difficult, an easy success in a single paper cannot be expected. But even the first paper usually represents an advance over the preceding work; moreover, it gives him experience and a better understanding of the functioning of his instruments, thus enabling him to devise further improvements in his apparatus, to undertake with it a second piece of research, and to report the complete understanding of all the secondary processes taking place in his set-up, if necessary, trying separate experiments to elucidate some obscure details. In this way the very sources of error become subjects of research, leading to instructive results, and sometimes to significant discoveries. Thus, by slow degrees Millikan advances to a complete mastery of every aspect of his problem and brings the investigation to a close, in the sense that he obtains final results which could not be improved upon with the experimental resources of the epoch.[112]

It is clear, too, from an examination of the evolution of Millikan's research, that his work was guided by strong theoretical commitments. Although he later liked to talk of his work in terms of dispassionate experiment, unguided by theoretical predispositions, his research was heavily charged with theory. In his Nobel Prize address he spoke of his electron work as a "test of the correctness or incorrectness of Benjamin Franklin's conception of a particle or an atom, of electricity,"[113] but it is clear that the existence and special characteristics of the electron were presupposed by his research program. In his photoelectric work he began, and finished, as a partisan of the wave theory of light: while he persisted in denying the essential quantum character of light, he saw his work as confirming the quantum character of emission processes. Millikan found—with elegance and precision—what he was looking for.

Millikan's efforts during the decade 1903–13, despite their earlier disappointing results and later successes, were all earnest attempts to confront the new situation in physics and are in their own way very revealing. His approach to the new physics in his experimental researches conforms to a pattern that remains consistent through his years of success leading to the Nobel Prize: Millikan was a conservative in the midst of a revolutionary world. If we choose to think of the revolutionary in science as one who seeks to probe, assess, and eventually undermine the secure foundations of orthodoxy, we may define the conservative as one who seeks to preserve as far as possible existing conventions. Millikan was one such scientist, and as a conservative physicist in a fluid and rapidly changing situation, Millikan always sought to establish secure benchmarks, and through orderly procedures and exact measurements to effect what he considered to be stable progress in physics.

Millikan's conservative credo was characteristically presented to the public only slowly, over half a decade, from 1912 to 1917. In an article published in *Popular Science Monthly* in May 1912, he made very clear his opposition to the revolutionary temperament:

> I wish vigorously to combat the point of view which I fear too many of those who are not engaged at first hand in scientific inquiry gain, both from the "revolutionary discoveries" which are continually being announced by the daily press, and also from the prominence which scientists themselves naturally give to the demolition of time-honored hypotheses in which they do not believe—the point of view that none of the theories of the scientists are after all any more than transient phenomena, that they are all just a part of the continual change and flux of things, that this generation discards wholesale all the hypotheses which were held adequate in the last and that the next generation will make equally short work of all the theories which today hold sway.

Opposing this view, Millikan held that "there are some things even in science which we may safely say that we *know*, that there are some theories which we may be reasonably certain are going to endure." What will endure is what we have measured: "There is no science without exact measurement. There may be good guesses at it, many plausible explanations, but no real knowledge." The so-called revolutions in science do not overthrow but rather complement what we already firmly know. "We do indeed discover new relations, but for the most part the old ones remain."[114] The key to this continuity is orderly procedure.

In an address before the American Institute of Electrical Engineers in February 1917, Millikan detailed his philosophy. The universe is "ultimately rationally intelligible" and is uniform. "It will have naught of caprice in nature." The scientific method captures this universe for us: "It is the method which believes in a minute, careful, wholly dispassionate analysis of a situation." Despite the advances in physics since 1895 and the seemingly revolutionary changes that had taken place, Millikan insisted that the "progress of science is almost never by the process of revolution.... They almost never happen." When the atom was found to have a structure and the whole subatomic region was opened to exploration, even this turn of events for Millikan was no revolution: "All that was above remained exactly as it had been, and no chemist had any occasion to be disturbed, for the chemists' laws were just as precise as they had been before.... The growth of science is in general by a process of accretion, almost never by revolution."[115] In the introduction to his classic book *The Electron*, Millikan put the same sentiment in this way: "A science, like a planet, grows in the main by a process of infinitesimal accretion. Each research is usually a modification of a preceding one; each new theory is built like a cathedral through the addition by many builders of many different elements."[116]

Millikan's conservatism also illuminates his serious interest in the history of science, which he later taught at the California Institute of Technology and to which he often referred in his writings. Millikan was one of thirty-seven members of the organizing committee of the History of Science Society in 1924 and continued his interest in the subject until his death.[117] For Millikan the history of science demonstrated the continuities in which he so firmly believed. "What we were trying to do," he later wrote of his textbooks, "was to show how to bring to every man some conception of the method and the history of physics and a realization of the social results that have followed from its development."[118] His last text, *New Elementary Physics* (1936), is organized around seven historical "units"; the history of physics, its gradual development and evolution, and the applications of its method are integrated into a course for the beginner which displays Millikan's view of the discipline.

Millikan's philosophical core, then, combined several elements: his view of scientific change, which demanded orderly progress and kept him suspicious of radical innovation; his conviction, drawn from Michelson and conforming to well-established American traditions in physics, that excellence was achieved through precise measurement; and his patient method of entering an established research program, gradually mastering its fine points, and finally wringing from it the last drop of scientific nectar. He managed to synthesize this mix of temperament and philosophy into an outstanding career.

Frank B. Jewett, Millikan's long-time friend and colleague, perceptively described Millikan's achievement in an essay that was never made public:

> I do not think Millikan is a great physicist in the sense that we look upon Newton, Kelvin, Helmholtz or J. J. Thomson, that is, as a man who has produced or will produce revolutionary ideas. His place is rather that of a great consolidator and experimenter, a man who is capable of gleaning by critical analysis from the suggestions of others those hypotheses which are most nearly correct, subjecting them to properly devised and carried out experimental verification and transforming them from the realm of hypothesis to the realm of exact proved fact.[119]

No more accurate assessment of Millikan's strengths has since appeared. But P. W. Bridgman also expressed a succinct and valuable appraisal in his review of Millikan's *Autobiography* in 1950. For Bridgman, the key to Millikan's success lay in his "exhuberant energy, and the vision that knew how to concentrate on the essential and the significant."[120]

Millikan's genius lay in what psychologists have called convergent thinking—channeled and controlled effort toward the unique answer. Convergent thinking is required in the area of compelling inferences, in deducing the one correct solution. Its counterpart, divergent thinking, is important for breaking new ground, supplying new kinds of answers to the conventional questions.[121] Millikan's greatness resulted not from a singular approach to experiment or theory but rather from his extraordinary skill in execution, his insight into experimental difficulties and techniques for overcoming them, and his undeniable patience and fortitude. He perfected and secured scientific paths that others had pioneered.

Millikan's conservatism generally carried over into all areas of his life. Politically, socially, and aesthetically he tended toward the conventional. In 1912 he was a Taft Republican, and later he became a staunch supporter of Herbert Hoover. He identified Republicanism with all that was progressive and decent; the Democrats he associated with the "corrupt, controlled vote of the city slums."[122] Socially, he believed in the primacy of what he termed the Anglo-Saxon race.[123] In art and architecture he decried "the thoroughly diseased state of mind that is found so often in modern art."[124] Millikan's career exemplifies what the psychologists J. W. Getzels and P. W. Jackson found in regard to other gifted, highly convergent minds: such people, they found, tend to "converge upon stereotyped meanings, to perceive personal success by conventional standards, to move towards the model provided by teachers, to seek out careers that conform to what is expected of them."[125]

The historiography of science has for good and obvious reasons concentrated on the revolutionaries in science—the divergent thinkers. Millikan's convergent research did, however, play an important part in the success of the revolution in physics, as exemplified by the complex role he performed in the ultimate success of the light quantum hypothesis and the wide employment of his measurements of e and h in modern physics. Such work, it has been argued, is essential for the occurrence of scientific revolutions. Thomas Kuhn has maintained that "flexibility and openmindedness have...been too exclusively emphasized as the characteristics requisite for basic research. ...Something like 'convergent thinking' is just as essential to scientific advance as is divergent."[126] The highly creative and conceptually innovative protagonists of the twentieth-century revolution in physics—Einstein, Niels Bohr, Erwin Schrödinger, Wolfgang Pauli, Werner Heisenberg, and the like—amply deserve the attention they have received and will continue to receive. Historians of science are obligated, however, to assay Kuhn's contention that "the productive scientist must be a traditionalist who enjoys playing games by pre-established rules in order to be a successful innovator who discovers new rules and new pieces with which to play them."[127] When taken as a description of the scientific community as a whole, as well as of the individual, this view offers suggestive insights for historians who, like the scientific community itself, are bewitched by the charm and excitement of the revolutionaries and therefore tend to underestimate the role of their cautions and reluctant colleagues. Millikan's search for order in the midst of revolution was a structural part of that change.

With the success of the new research programs, Millikan's star began to ascend rapidly in the world of science. He was promoted to the rank of full professor at the University of Chicago in 1910 and received his first honorary doctorate from his alma mater, Oberlin, in 1911. The year 1913, however, initiated the pouring forth of honors. Beginning with Northwestern in 1913, he received by 1917 four more honorary doctorates, all from prestigious universities. He was awarded the Comstock Prize of the National Academy of Sciences in 1913 and was elected in rapid succession to the American Philosophical Society (1913), the American Academy of Arts and Sciences (1914), and the National Academy of Sciences (1915), and to the presidency of the American Physical Society (1915). By the time of America's entrance into World War I, Millikan was without question one of America's best known and most widely respected physicists. His rise was stunning; P. W. Bridgman recalled the "question which so puzzled or even dismayed the physicists of a generation ago; how was it possible that a man comparatively unheard of and with no recognized achievement in research should suddenly blossom out at the age of 45 into a physicist of the first magnitude?"[128] The problem admits of no simple answer, but surely involves Millikan's keen eye for the critically significant problems, his developing sense of the practicable, and his indefatigable diligence. His critical choice at age forty to serve modern physics' most pressing problems and at the same time to remain true to prevailing American standards of excellence—that is, to become the "physicist of the sixth decimal place" prophesied by Michelson—was both appropriate and wise. That decision thrust him to the center of the stage of world physics.

His new fame was partly bound, with piquant irony, to the Einstein boom of 1919 and after. With the results of the eclipse expedition of that year, which supported his remarkable views of gravitation, Einstein became a public figure—a famous man. Moreover, among physicists, the almost universal skepticism that had met his concept of the light quantum or photon had begun to soften, partly because of the efforts of Emil Warburg in photochemistry and (paradoxically) the work of opponents of the photon concept, such as Millikan and William Duane. But by 1923, when Millikan was awarded the Nobel Prize for Physics, he himself still retained his fundamental skepticism about the localization of light in the photon.

When Einstein received the Nobel Prize in Physics for 1921, the award was given "especially for his discovery of the law of the photoelectric effect." In his presentation speech, the famous Swedish chemist Svante Arrhenius noted that "Einstein's law of the photo-electrical effect has been extremely rigorously tested by the American Millikan and his pupils and passed the test brilliantly."[129] At the Nobel ceremony for Millikan in May 1924, Professor Allvar Gullstrand of the Royal Swedish Academy of Sciences insisted that "if these researches of Millikan [on the photoelectric effect] had given a different result, the law of Einstein would have been without value, and the theory of Bohr without support. After Millikan's results both were awarded a Nobel Prize for Physics."[130] Millikan was still reluctant to acknowledge the existence of the photon. In his own acceptance address, Millikan responded with the proper mixture of pride and humility. "At the present time," he said, "it is not too much to say that the altogether overwhelming proof furnished by many different observers...that Einstein's equation is of exact validity...and of very general applicability, is perhaps the most conspicuous achievement of Experimental Physics during the past decade." But, he continued, "the conception of *localized* light-quanta out of which Einstein got his equation must still be regarded as far from being established.... Until it can account for the facts of interference and the other effects which have seemed thus far to be irreconcilable with it, we must withhold our full assent. Possibly the recent steps taken by Duane, Compton, Epstein and Ehrenfest may ultimately bear fruit in bringing even interference under the control of localized light-quanta. But as yet the path is dark."[131]

In his Faraday lecture before the Chemical Society in London, Millikan spent more time discussing the work of A. H. Compton, the so-called Compton effect, and its confirmation by his own co-workers J. A. Becker, E. C. Watson, and W. R. Smythe,[132] along with the theoretical backing of his co-workers, Paul Epstein and Paul Ehrenfest for the photon.[133] He was able to state:

> It is then not merely the Einstein equation which is now having extraordinary successes, but the Einstein conception as well, for it was certainly out of this conception, whether it is right or wrong, that Compton got his equation. Possibly too Duane, Compton, Epstein and Ehrenfest in recent papers are making a little progress towards removing the apparent contradiction with interference, but the way is yet very dark. The times are, however, pregnant with new ideas, and atomic conceptions in the field of ether waves seem to hold at the moment the master-key to progress.[134]

The metaphor of gestation with regard to the emergence of scientific ideas is, of course, no accident. As we have seen, Millikan was committed to a smooth, not a disruptive, curve of progress in science. Science walks, not races, ahead. In his Nobel Prize speech, he described his view of the process:

> The fact that Science walks forward on two feet, namely theory and experiment, is nowhere better illustrated than in the two fields for slight contributions to which you have done me the great honour of awarding me the Nobel Prize in Physics for the year 1923. Sometimes it is one foot which is put forward first, sometimes the other, but continuous progress is only made by the use

of both—by theorizing and then testing, or by finding new relations in the process of experimenting and then bringing the theoretical foot up and pushing it on beyond, and so on in unending alternations.[135]

He saw himself as a progressive-conservative, for in his view, "the history of physics has clearly demonstrated that the middle course between devotion to the new and the worship of the already discovered truth is the only correct one for the progress of physics"—or, more succinctly, "the only real progressive is in the center."[136]

Philosophers of science may quarrel with Millikan's assessment of the nature of scientific change, but few will argue about the appropriateness of his self-perception; he described his own career acutely indeed.

4

The Scientist in Action

> All that other folks can do,
> Why, with patience, should not you?
> Only keep this rule in view:
>   Try, try again.
>   —*McGuffey's Reader*

By 1916 Millikan the research scientist had moved to the center of the world stage. During the next two decades he assumed new roles: consultant, director of laboratories, chief executive of a major institution of higher learning and representative of the scientific community to the public. His scientific and professional life became intricately intertwined with two others, those of the astrophysicist George Ellery Hale and the physical chemist Arthur A. Noyes. This triumvirate was responsible for the rapid rise to prominence of a bright new star in America's scientific firmament, the California Institute of Technology (Caltech). These three colleagues became widely influential in American science. They painstakingly built a network of personal and scientific relations that enabled them to mobilize resources for research and to use them effectively. They were key figures in a scientific establishment that aimed to bring the United States to world leadership in science.

Millikan first became acquainted with George Hale in August 1897, when, as a young University of Chicago instructor, he was invited to attend a reception honoring the opening of Hale's new observatory.[1] The relationship between the two young men—a partnership that was to prove exceedingly fruitful—did not, however, take root for another decade and a half.

By the time they came together again, just before America's

entry into World War I, Millikan was a full professor, an internationally respected researcher, and a major force in American science. Hale was the director of the premier American solar observatory, a powerful member of the National Academy, and in general an ambitious scientific planner. Millikan wrote to his wife, Greta, "[Hale] is the most *restless* flea on the American continent—more things *eating him* than I could tell you about in an hour."[2]

This "restless flea" is most often remembered for his invention and development of the spectroheliograph, for his investigations of sun spots, prominences, and the chromosphere, for his proof of the existence of a magnetic field in the sun, and above all for his organizational and promotional ability. He was responsible for the construction of the Mount Wilson Observatory, which he directed for many years, and for the Mount Palomar 200-inch telescope. He was a plotter, a planner, in his own eyes a hatcher of schemes. World War I gave Hale what he saw as a great opportunity. "I really believe," he wrote to an associate in 1916, "this is the greatest chance we have ever had to advance research in America. The spirit of national service in the air coupled with the desire for preparedness should make everything possible."[3]

Seizing his chance, Hale began to develop new institutional forms for science in America, and a mainstay of his new establishment was the rising young physicist Robert Millikan. At Hale's patriotic urging, the National Academy of Sciences offered its services to the nation; the result—Hale's brainchild—was the National Service Research Foundation, later renamed the National Research Council (NRC).

Millikan played a key role in Hale's Research Council plans. In April 1916 he was named to the organizing committee of what was soon to become the NRC, along with Hale himself, Arthur Amos Noyes, and the physician Simon Flexner. Later that year Millikan was appointed to the Executive Committee of the council. In June, when Hale and Noyes visited Millikan at the Ryerson, they showed deep interest in his work on the photoelectric effect and his oil-drop experiments, as well as in enlisting his support for their efforts to organize American scientists.[4]

Hale made a tremendous impression on Millikan. While he was in New York to teach at Columbia's summer session, Millikan met with Hale and John Joseph Carty, of the American Telephone and Telegraph Company, and wrote to Greta: "Yesterday George Hale and Carty both got hold of me and we had a day of it.... Among many other things he wants me to spend three months of each year in Pasadena starting a new physical laboratory there. Then he wants to start a new popular science journal which I opposed."[5]

Hale had long concerned himself with the advancement of science in the United States, and especially with the role of the National Academy of Sciences, to which he had been elected in 1902. In a series of articles that appeared in *Science* from 1913 to 1915, Hale pushed for expansion of the academy's role in American science. "It is safe to predict," Hale wrote, "that the privilege of securing the Academy's aid in the control and disbursement of large sums for the benefit of science will be widely sought in the future."[6]

The National Academy of Sciences was founded in 1863, by an act of Congress, for the purpose of providing scientific advice sought by government agencies. In the years between the Civil War and World War I the academy received few requests for its services. Membership was an acknowledgment of prestige but did not confer access to power. Hale, however, saw in the academy a body around which scientific research interests of all types—industrial and academic as well as governmental—could be organized. Yet, like most members, he feared the political ties that might bind and damage its independence. Much of the ensuing history of the academy's science politics is the story of Hale's skillful attempts to steer a course between the Scylla of government interference and the Charybdis of the scientific community's traditional lack of money and power.

The sinking of the *Lusitania* gave Hale his opportunity to use the academy to attain his goals and at the same time increased the risk of closer links with the government. In a day letter dated July 13, 1915, Hale told the academy's president, William H. Welch, of The Johns Hopkins University, that "further reflection and conference... convinces me that the Academy is under strong obligations to offer services to the President in the event of war with Mexico or Germany."[7] Welch was hesitant. He believed that Hale's plan had to be considered by the academy's council, a difficult task to arrange in midsummer. "I can imagine," he replied, "no objection to the Academy offering its services to the President in the event of war—I think an improbable event while Wilson is president—but I am not clear about our organizing a committee at present."[8]

The urgency of Hale's concern may have stemmed from his fear that the academy would be eclipsed as technical adviser to the government by Thomas A. Edison's Naval Consulting Board. In July 1915, Secretary of the Navy Josephus Daniels had asked Edison to head a board that would work to organize American inventiveness with regard to naval warfare, with special emphasis on such new possibilities as submarine attack. On July 13 Edison's personal representative advised Daniels of Edison's acceptance, and the board, completely independent of the National Academy of Sciences, was constituted.[9] Hale suggested to Welch that "to disarm possible criticism and assure success we should concentrate on medicine and surgery but include representatives of other subjects on the committee. Daniels' announcement today regarding Edison confirms this."[10] After the sinking of the *Sussex* in March 1916 and President Wilson's ultimatum to Germany in April, the National Academy of Sciences, at Hale's urging, officially offered its services to the nation. The immediate result was the formation of the National Research Council (NRC), with representatives from industry, education, scientific societies, and government agencies. In some sense a child of "preparedness," the NRC quickly became an effective body when war began.[11]

The coming of the war and the preparedness theme thus provided the occasion for, but not the source of, the established scientists' concern with systematizing research and its relations with other institutions of society. By the end of 1913 the American Academy for the Advancement of Science (AAAS) had organized the Committee of One Hundred to promote scientific research in America. At a meeting at the Cosmos Club in Washington, D.C., in April 1914, leading members of the AAAS, including A. A. Noyes, Hale, J. McKeen Cattell, E. C. Pickering, and Ira Remsen, discussed such questions as the feasibility of a central bureau for research under the AAAS, the National Academy of Sciences, or the Smithsonian Institution; research in industry and educational institutions; and the selection and preparation of scientists.[12] Committees were formed, meetings held annually for several years, and reports published. One of the most impressive of these reports was C. E. K. Mees's "Organization of Industrial Research Laboratories," in which he argued on behalf of the Committee of One Hundred that "for industries to retain their position and make progress they must earnestly devote time and money to the investigation of the fundamental theory underlying the subject in which they are interested."[13]

The committee rapidly became obsolescent as the war progressed and as the National Research Council grew in importance. Indeed, the mainstays of the NRC—including Millikan, Carty, J. C. Merriam, Hale, Noyes, Robert M. Yerkes, James R. Angell, and C. D. Walcott—were also at the heart of the Committee of One Hundred. In any case, the National Academy of Sciences and its daughter, the NRC, increasingly held center stage. The NRC, in fact, later claimed the leading role in advancing the interests of scientific research in peacetime America. Under the effective leadership of Hale, Millikan, Noyes, Carty, Gano Dunn, and others allied with them, the NRC pressed for an executive order to make the body a permanent part of the academy. President Wilson signed such an order in May 1918.[14]

Early in 1917 both Millikan and Hale decided to take leave from their civilian employment and aid the preparedness effort. In March Millikan was appointed head of an NRC subcommittee on submarine detection, and his appointees to the committee included Ernest Merritt of Cornell, William F. Durand of Stanford, Robert Wood of Johns Hopkins, Irving Langmuir of General Electric, Frank Jewett of Western Electric, and C. E. Mendenhall of Wisconsin. Millikan was excited by the possibility of putting science to work, of demonstrating the worth of scientific expertise to the public at large. In April 1917 he wrote to Greta from Washington, D.C., "This much is clear. If the science men of the country are going to be of any use to her it is now or never. The next three months will decide whether we can perfect an organization which will keep us abreast of foreign governments in the utilization of expert scientific knowledge possessed by the country or whether we cannot."[15]

Millikan's opportunity to act came quickly. In June 1917 General George Squier, chief of the Army Signal Corps and the holder of a Ph.D. in physics from Johns Hopkins, asked Millikan to join the army as head of the Signal Corps's Science and Research Division. Squier's cajoling and Hale's urging overcame Millikan's initial reluctance. He was commissioned a major, and later rose to the rank of lieutenant colonel.[16]

During the same month, the New London Experiment Station was organized to develop antisubmarine devices. Its members included such physicists as Merritt of Cornell, H. A. Wilson of Rice, Max Mason of Wisconsin, G. W. Pierce and P. W. Bridgman of Harvard, and Henry Bumstead, E. F. Nichols, and John Zeleny of Yale. Out of this group came the Mason device, an adaptation of a French instrument and similar in principle to the stethoscope, which was able to detect moving submarines at distances of up to ten miles.[17]

Millikan was also intimately connected with the meteorological division of the Signal Corps, especially with its efforts to distribute propaganda via long-range pilot balloons.[18] His experience with ballooning was to be of significant service later in his cosmic-ray work.

The concern of Millikan, Hale and their colleagues on the National Research Council to demonstrate to the nation at large what Millikan called "the utilization of expert scientific knowledge" was amply satisfied by the end of the war. To consolidate their gains, Hale and the others acted quickly to confirm the NRC as a peacetime science agency, and began to national educational effort to spread the twin gospel of science and efficiency.

A remarkable book published in 1920, *The New World of Science,* epitomizes the NRC effort. The editor was Robert Yerkes, the distinguished psychologist, and then chairman of the NRC's Research Information Service. Contributors included Hale, Millikan, A. A. Noyes, James R. Angell, Clarence West

Lieutenant Colonel Millikan and Max. Courtesy of the Archives, California Institute of Technology.

of the Chemical Warfare Service, A. E. Kennelly, and others. Hale's introduction was blunt and direct: "One of the most striking results of the war is the emphasis it has laid on the national importance of science and research." But Hale became eloquent at the integral character of the science-society relationship:

> Our place in the industrial world, the advance of our commerce, the health of our people, the output of our farms, the conditions under which the great majority of our population must labor, and the security of the nation will thus depend, in large and increasing measure, on the attention we devote to the promotion of scientific and industrial research. The purpose of this book is therefore to describe the part played by science in the war with special reference to future development and utilization of research on a scale commensurate with the needs of the United States.[19]

Millikan contributed two articles to the book, "The Contributions of Physical Science" and "Some Scientific Aspects of the Meterological Work of the United States Army," a reprint of an article that had appeared the previous year. But the most vivid insight into Millikan's thinking on the relationship between science and society at the close of the war is provided by an address he delivered at the University of Chicago and published in *Science*, the organ of the American Association for the Advancement of Science, on September 26, 1919. Titled "The New Opportunity in Science," the address explored in some detail "the situations created by the war" and "the lessons taught by it."[20]

Although science and technology were no strangers to the conduct of war, scientists were justified in claiming that, for the first time, science had transformed the character of warfare and had become indispensable to it. Physical scientists and engineers introduced and developed such powerful tools as sound ranging (locating the position of gun batteries by computing the centers of sound waves emanating from them), submarine detection devices, accurate bomb-dropping techniques, aerial photography, aeronautic instrumentation, radiotelephony, wireless communication between airplanes, and infrared and ultraviolet signaling.[21] The meterological section of the army's

Science and Research Division developed long-range propaganda-carrying balloons, drew more sophisticated and complete maps of the upper regions of the atmosphere to facilitate aerial navigation, and developed aids to artillery.[22] The Chemical Warfare Service greatly increased the United States' capabilities for gas warfare by developing new antipersonnel gases and gas masks. Clarence West described the service's "crowning achievement" as the introduction of mustard gas, a blistering gas that can cause casualties up to ten days after its shell has been fired.[23] The Ordnance Department, under astronomer F. R. Moulton, created new methods for computing projectile trajectories and better tables to correct for "ballistic wind."[24]

The many impressive applications of scientific talent to war led Millikan to assert, rather extravagantly, that

> for the first time in history the world has been waked up by the war to an appreciation of what science can do. But just now the War has taught young soldiers that they need their science for success. Administrative positions in the industries are to-day being filled as never before from the ranks of the technically trained men. The War has taught the prospective officer that he can not hope for promotion unless he has scientific training. The War has taught the manufacturer that he can not hope to keep in the lead of his industry save through the brains of a research group, which alone can keep him in the forefront of progress. As a result of all this there is indeed a new opportunity in every phase and branch of science.[25]

This new opportunity merely reflected changes in society that had slowly been taking place since the Civil War. World War I had caused these changes—in government, industry, and even academic life—to reveal themselves in an amazingly sharp, clear light and had even quickened them. The expanding importance within American society of trained specialists and the increasing power and prestige of science itself were now widely recognized.[26] Thus, if World War I did not call into being America's "technostructure"[27] or even alter the direction of its course, it did in fact focus attention on the expanded role of scientists in society, and it imbued scientists with a new confidence and a sense of a destiny soon to be realized. After the fashion of research groups in the war effort, well-trained scientific men were being mobilized in industry. "The Ph.D. in physics, if he is a man of ability, is in demand today in the industries as he has never been before." Experimental work, for the first time in an important way, was opening to team effort. The day of the isolated experimenter was near an end; "the war has demonstrated the immense advantage of co-operation." A young American seeking a vocation must be encouraged to consider science: "...the scientist is, in the broad sense, a creator of wealth as truly as is the man whose attention is focused on the application of science. Indeed, the scientist is merely the scout, the explorer who is sent on ahead to discover and open up new leads to nature's gold."[28]

Millikan also saw a new opportunity for people who already possessed wealth to invest in the scientific enterprise, for no better investment existed. The fact that the United States had not been the leading scientific nation was due not to a lack of natural abilities or even of facilities, but rather to a lack of determination on the part of its superior young men to choose science as a career. "Our greatest need is not for more facilities, but for the selection and development of men of outstanding ability in science. Find a way to select and develop men, and results will take care of themselves."[29]

It was not through government initiative that this development would come about; such "socialism" was anathema to Millikan. In America, private initiative might be summoned to the task of creating research chairs and centers: "Most of our great advances in the past have been through private initiative and I suspect Mr. Elihu Root was, as usual, a wise counselor when he said recently, in substance, 'If we are going to conserve the finest elements in Anglo-Saxon civilization, we must conserve the method of the private initiative and not depend primarily upon government aid.'"[30]

The lessons the war taught science—the importance of scientific research for the nation's economy and security and the importance of cooperative efforts for the scientific enterprise itself—were grafted on a legacy of nineteenth-century liberalism. The result was a paradox. Whereas such scientists as Millikan and Hale doubtless felt the lure of government intervention, with all the resources and power it would bring, they feared government control or interference and remained steadfast in their faith in the altruism of American business leaders and the ultimate social wisdom of development along lines laid down by American individualism.[31]

Millikan emerged from his wartime and NRC experience to find himself in a vastly different situation. In 1917 he was a well-respected teacher and researcher, with the peach glow of success surrounding his experimental investigations and with a growing national and international reputation. Two years later he was well embedded in very influential networks, a powerful ally of the indefatigable Hale, and at age fifty on the threshold of power and influence.

At this point the lives of Millikan and Hale became even more closely intertwined. Hale was the key figure in the creation of a tremendously successful scientific-cultural complex in Pasadena, California—a complex that includes the California Institute of Technology (Caltech), the Mount Wilson Observatory, and the Huntington Library and Museum. He wanted—and got—Millikan as Caltech's first president, or, as his exact title read, Chairman of the Executive Council.

The story of Hale's decade-long plan to create Caltech is tortuous but necessary for our examination of Millikan's rise, for the stories are inseparable. Hale provides an interesting counterpoint for Millikan, both personally and professionally. Frank Jewett of the American Telephone and Telegraph Company, who knew both men intimately, perceptively characterized Millikan as a remarkable "field general"—a man with a shrewd sense of tactics who could implement complex plans—and Hale as a gifted strategist.[32] Hale was by nature a planner of what he liked to call "schemes"; the ample historical record demonstrates his success at schemes and the inner consistency of his strategy. The key to understanding the early scientific excellence of Caltech is to understand Hale's perception of the scientific and institutional needs of astrophysics. This perception formed the basis of his strategy to create a new kind of research organization at Caltech.

When Hale first became interested in science, astronomers were still largely concerned with positional rather than physical questions, that is, with increasing the precision of measurement of stellar positions and parallax and of double stars.[33] Hale's early scientific heroes, however, were such physical astronomers–astrophysicists as William Huggins and Norman Lockyer, who used the spectroscope to study the constitution of the sun and stars. In unpublished autobiographical notes, Hale described his introduction to the spectroscope: "My delight in science did not reach its peak until [1883, when] I first learned about the spectroscope. Keenly as I had been interested in all that had gone before, I was completely carried off my feet when I began to appreciate some of the possibilities of this extraordinary instrument. From that moment my fate was sealed."[34] Students of scientific biography may recognize in Hale's recollection a familiar moment when a complex of ideas and circumstances come together to form a perception that profoundly influences a scientist's professional life. Hale's early delight in and enthusiasm for the spectroscope and in general his enthusiasm for the application of physics and chemistry to astronomy guided his mature work, both scientific and organizational.

Two excerpts from Hale's writings, the first from 1899 and the second from 1929, indicate the intensity and the persistence of his vision:

A new science has sprung up which offers problems not to be solved by the astronomer alone, but only by the combined skill of the astronomer, the physicist and the chemist. The votary of the new astronomy...watching in laboratory the vibrations of the molecule in the Bunsen flame or electric arc...registers visible and even invisible phenomena upon the photographic plate, and then, comparing his work with the photographic record of stellar or solar vibrations he is able to reason with clearness and certainty upon the constitution of heavenly bodies.[35]

I was thus bound to undertake the heavy task of raising funds or to forgo the possibilities I seemed to see ahead. These were nothing less than an effective union of astronomy and physics, directed primarily toward the solution of the problem of stellar evolution but with equal advantages to be gained by fundamental physics from such a joint study.[36]

Hale's vision of creating resources for research to join physics, chemistry, and astronomy originated with his early enthusiasm over the scientific possibilities of the spectroscope and ended with the organizational achievements of Mount Palomar and Caltech.

By the time Hale entered the Massachusetts Institute of Technology in 1886, he had already designed and constructed a spectroscopic laboratory near his home in Chicago, and he returned to it after graduation. Here he used his recently invented spectroheliograph to observe solar prominences and sunspots. He soon began to plan schemes. He induced friends and acquaintances to contribute to the Yerkes Observatory, which was established in 1897 at Williams Bay, Wisconsin, and of which he became the director, and he arranged to have the University of Chicago provide an annual subsidy of $1,000 for his new *Astrophysical Journal*.[37] The journal sought to unite the literature on the use of the spectroscope in chemistry, physics, and astronomy; its scope extended to "all investigations of radiant energy."[38] In 1899 Hale founded the American Association of Astronomers and Astrophysicists.[39] In all of these schemes Hale pursued his great ideal of cooperative research.[40]

Specialized training and research interests of scientists during the late nineteenth and early twentieth centuries resulted in a peculiar situation; as scientists became more deeply concerned with special problems, they become more dependent on scientists in other specialties. Nature, it seemed, was not divided according to rigid academic disciplines; physicists required new mathematical techniques, astronomers required the results of research in physics and chemistry, physiologists needed those of organic chemistry, and chemists those of physics. By the early twentieth century, scientific disciplines began to demand assistance from their neighbors, and common questions were approached from both sides of a disciplinary barrier. Traditional disciplinary lines were crossed and new sciences developed—astrophysics, biochemistry, physical chemistry, and the like. The merging of disciplines was accelerated by the introduction of powerful new instruments such as the spectroscope, the full exploitation of which required the efforts of chemists, physicists, and astronomers. Hale believed not only that astronomers would benefit by using the laboratory methods and results of the physical scientists, but that their cooperation would benefit chemists and physicists as well. He observed in 1904: "The solar observer may be the spectator of physical and chemical experiments on a scale far transcending any that can ever be performed in the laboratory. In this enormous crucible, heated to temperatures greatly exceeding those attainable by artificial means, immense masses of luminous vapor...may be seen undergoing changes and transformations well calculated to assist in the explanation of problems which the laboratory cannot solve."[41] More clearly than most others of his generation, Hale saw that the new opportunities for cooperative research would place new demands on the social organization of science. The new astronomy that attracted him in the 1880s required a reordering of scientific research in the twentieth century.

By the fall of 1901 Hale was engaged in a scheme to establish an observatory at the Massachusetts Institute of Technology which would be coordinated with Noyes's projected Department of Chemical Research there.[42] His first opportunity came, however, with the founding of the Carnegie Institution of Washington. "I remember...vividly," Hale later remarked, "the newspaper paragraph in 1902 stating that Andrew Carnegie had given a fund of 10 million dollars for the creation of an institution solely devoted to research."[43] It "seemed almost too good to be true."[44] Owing to the limitations of geography and of institutional financing, Hale was already disappointed with the Yerkes Observatory, and he looked to the Carnegie Institution to establish a new observatory. As a member of the Carnegie Institution's Advisory Committee on astronomy, he allied himself with the executive secretary of the institution, Charles D. Walcott, who supported his plans for a new facility. Like Hale, Walcott was an admirer of "the modern idea of cooperation and community of effort"; he wrote to Andrew Carnegie in 1903 that they "might as well try to make a great research institution of the C.I. by pure individualism as to expect success in great industrial enterprises by the individualism of 1850–1870."[45] Hale was designated as the prospective head of the new observatory.[46] He wanted a solar observatory to be located in a favorable climate, and on his advice Mount Wilson, near Pasadena, California, was selected late in 1903.

The time was auspicious for solar physics. The invention of spectroheliography by Hale (and independently by Henri Deslandres in France) enabled astronomers to obtain pictures of the sun from the light of its various elements. The study of solar prominences, for example, which had been restricted to eclipses, now became routine. In general, the excellent solar images opened up new areas for research. Hale, a self-confessed "sun worshiper," continued the solar research he had begun at Yerkes.[47]

The new observatory not only provided Hale with superb equipment and relatively ample financing, but also permitted him new freedom in organizing research. It became a working model of the interdisciplinary research ideal about which he and Noyes had earlier corresponded. At first Hale lacked a telescope comparable to the one at Yerkes, but he soon obtained funds for one from John D. Hooker, a Los Angeles business-man and amateur astronomer, and from the Carnegie Institu-tion. In 1908 a sixty-inch reflecting telescope was installed atop Mount Wilson. As one of his first priorities Hale established a physical laboratory and related machine shops on Mount Wilson and in Pasadena. Here he produced comparison spectra with an electric furnace, and other researchers investigated the effects of magnetic and electric fields and of temperature and pressure on spectral lines. Using electric furnaces, pressure pumps, and other physical apparatus, Hale and his co-workers imitated solar and stellar phenomena.[48] Hale brought the phys-icists C. G. Abbot, Henry Gale, and E. F. Nichols to Mount Wilson for radiation studies, and he hired Arthur S. King (one of Berkeley's first Ph.D.s in physics) to head the physics labora-tory. He invited distinguished visitors such as A. A. Michelson and the Dutch astronomer J. C. Kapteyn, partly in an effort to induce younger scientists to come to work there.[49] Hale also hoped to build up chemical researches in connection with Mount Wilson. "It happens," he later wrote to Walcott, "that certain of our problems, such as the improvement of photo-graphic plates and various questions of solar and stellar chemis-try could be very greatly advanced through cooperation with [a chemical] laboratory.... I need hardly say that Noyes would be an ideal man for the place."[50]

Already successful, Hale generated yet more schemes. In 1907 he was invited to join several distinguished Pasadena residents as a trustee of a local manual training school, Throop Polytechnic Institute. Throop might seem to have little to recommend it as a locus for Hale's ambitious plans, for it had an unimpressive physical plant and unimpressive personnel. But it had an asset that Hale was eager to seize upon: a board of trustees of influential men who could, and in the next decade eventually would, provide entrée to Los Angeles' rich and powerful. In 1907 Hale persuaded the board of trustees to drop the elementary parts of the school and retain only a college of engineering offering bachelor's degrees. In the following year the presidency fell vacant and Hale arranged the appointment of his acquaintance James Scherer.[51]

In 1908 Noyes was offered the chairmanship of the University of California's chemistry department and wrote to seek Hale's advice. Hale cautioned against the move: "You have built up [at M.I.T.] the most successful laboratory of chemical research in the United States if not in the world. Its great success depends upon you and no one else could maintain it in its present condition. Moreover you are in the midst of the scientific life of the country and can exert a strong influence ... which would necessarily be greatly diminished if you lived in California." Almost immediately Hale regretted his advice. He wrote again to Noyes to resurrect their old idea of collaboration and to offer him the choice of a deanship or a chemical research position at Throop. Noyes refused, but he did not rule out later reconsideration: "Perhaps another winter I might get out to Pasadena for a week of two and study the situation with you on the ground."[52]

Throop was still too modest to acquire the services of the director of chemical research and past acting president of M.I.T., and Hale returned to strengthening Mount Wilson. Noyes was willing to aid in the effort both out of friendship and out of concern with Hale's plans. By the spring of 1912, Hale and Noyes were planning to ask the Carnegie Institution to finance a physics laboratory in connection with the Mount

Wilson Observatory. Hale reported that R. S. Woodward, president of the Carnegie Institution, favored their plan and their suggestion that the University of Chicago's Millikan be invited to serve as its director. Noyes encouraged Hale: "I think your idea of suggesting Milliken [sic] to him was excellent. It will probably appeal to Woodward; and Milliken would be a great addition to the research staff. I should think that there might be a good chance to get him to come to such a laboratory as we propose."[53] Millikan was a clever choice, for among other reasons he was Woodward's former student and friend. Woodward was indeed pleased: "Such a combination," he wrote to Hale, "would form a company worthy of the great problems to be attacked."[54]

At about the same time Hale suggested to Woodward that they found a laboratory for physical chemistry in Pasadena with Noyes as its head. "The idea," Hale wrote, was "to get A. A. Noyes to take charge of a department of research in physical chemistry with a laboratory in Pasadena not connected with the Observatory but planned so as to cooperate with it, to the mutual advantage of both. My experience is that by working in this way the value of a given piece of research may often be doubled." Although this initiative failed because of Carnegie financial setbacks, the foundation of future success was laid.[55]

Hale had several reasons for selecting Noyes and Millikan. Noyes was compatible with Hale socially, personally, and scientifically. Hale and Noyes were approximately the same age and shared what Millikan was later fond of extolling as "Anglo-Saxon" roots. By the beginning of the century both were comparatively well-to-do and moved easily among the wealthy. Hale knew Noyes well, and he always preferred to rely on his friends. More important, however, Noyes shared Hale's views about cooperative research. Although Noyes viewed the blurring of disciplinary lines from the perspective of a physical chemist, their basic viewpoints were the same. Both felt that the really important scientific questions should be attacked jointly, by interdisciplinary collaboration.

Millikan, too, was compatible. He was Hale's age; the two first met at the official opening of the Yerkes Observatory, to which Millikan, then a new faculty member at the University of

Chicago, was invited.[56] As a student of Michael Pupin and Woodward at Columbia and as a colleague of Michelson, Millikan was well connected in scientific circles. His publications on the problems of radiation had attracted Hale's attention. He also had examined fundamental problems of matter, research that ultimately brought him the Nobel Prize. Even without the advantage of hindsight, Millikan, like Noyes, was a good choice.

Hale was persistent. In March and April 1913 he again attempted to persuade Noyes to come to Throop, if only on a part-time basis, to help plan a new laboratory. Even as these negotiations were under way, Hale made another attempt to interest the Carnegie Institution in a chemistry laboratory for Noyes, which he had recast as a "Chemical Energetics Laboratory." But this initiative, too, fell through.[57]

When Noyes finally arrived at Throop late in the fall of 1915, the irrepressible Hale was ready for the next step: "Noyes is now here," he wrote to his friend W. W. Campbell; "the plans are ready for his chemical laboratory with its large research division, and construction will begin at once. Our next attempt will be to secure funds for a physical laboratory with an equally good man at the head and similar provisions for research."[58] Events moved quickly, even for Hale. America's preparations for war and the war itself provided Hale with unexpected opportunities. His plans for the promotion of research in America, for reform of the National Academy of Sciences, and for the advancement of Throop (by then the Throop College of Technology) converged.

Hale's exuberant letter to Scherer at Throop on May 3, 1916, clearly shows how he brought together all his concerns: "I really believe this is the greatest chance we have ever had to advance research in America. The spirit of national service in the air coupled with the desire for preparedness should make everything possible. . . . *And I am going to give Throop the chance to lead the way.*" Even plans for the National Research Council did not divert Hale from his plan to create a physics laboratory in Pasadena with Millikan at its head: "If someone would provide a physical laboratory and fund physics! Millikan is coming to see me today about organizing the work of our committee in physics—I haven't broached the Throop scheme to him yet but am only waiting for a favorable opportunity. If we should ever get him for half the year Throop would have some part in the direction of American research."[59]

Even before the war Hale had begun to mount a campaign to attract Millikan to Throop. He urged him against accepting a handsome offer from Columbia, encouraging him instead to come part-time to Throop. He reported to Scherer that Millikan had a "great scheme to build up a sort of Woods Hole summer group of investigators in physics either here or in Chicago."[60] He wrote to Harry Pratt Judson, president of the University of Chicago, that he was trying to draw Millikan to Pasadena for such a project.[61]

At Throop, President Scherer (who was soon to retire) was busily assembling a major endowment for Millikan's possible shift to Pasadena.[62] Meanwhile Noyes's new laboratory—named the Gates Chemical Laboratory after its donors, C. W. Gates and P. G. Gates—opened in January 1917, and Millikan was induced, partly by a fund of $200,000 for his research work, to agree to spend three months of the year at Throop. Hale wrote to Woodward in January 1917: "He and Noyes and I are going to work out a cooperative plan for the study of electron problems from the physical, chemical and astronomical sides."[63]

The game was afoot—the cooperative plan of research that was to bear fruit after the war when all three were comfortably installed at Throop, now renamed the California Institute of Technology. Of this joint effort we shall hear more.

Now that both Millikan and Noyes were secured for Throop at least part-time, Hale moved to realize his broader aims. The story of his efforts to secure a building for the National Academy of Sciences and the National Research Council with Carnegie funds is well known.[64] By March 1918 he had completed an additional plan to secure Rockefeller money to establish research laboratories at three educational institutions: one in Chicago, one in the eastern part of the nation, and one in California. In explaining the plan to Arthur Fleming, a trustee and benefactor of Throop, Hale reported: "Colonel Millikan and I feel that the best place for the California headquarters would be Throop College of Technology."[65] By the fall of 1918 he had coordinated his views with those of Simon Flexner, an advocate of a strong central laboratory, to provide for a central research organization and three academic laboratories, all to be sponsored by the Rockefeller Foundation.[66]

During the following year, 1919, Hale was hard at work trying to secure matching money from Throop. He approached Norman Bridge, a wealthy retired physician, for an endowment and for funds for a physical laboratory. In his appeal he stressed that "both Michelson and Millikan" would be associated with it.[67] Bridge gave more than a quarter of a million dollars to establish the Norman Bridge Laboratory of Physics.

At the urging of Hale and with great reluctance, Noyes broke away completely from the Massachusetts Institute of Technology in 1919.[68] The plan for Rockefeller support for laboratories stalled, and Hale intensified his search for local money with an eye of luring Millikan to Pasadena as full-time president; the institution was to be renamed, at Noyes's insistence, the California Institute of Technology.[69] On hearing of the University of Chicago's intention to supply Millikan with an institute of his own, Hale candidly wrote Millikan: "I cannot easily give up the idea of establishing a great research laboratory of physics here, with you at its head."[70]

Millikan was still as reluctant as Noyes had been to make more than a part-time commitment to Pasadena. In turning down feelers from the University of California, Millikan wrote G. N. Lewis, "[I]t is not very likely that I shall feel it either *wise* or right for me to leave Chicago."[71] Hale put together a new offer. He told Henry Robinson, an influential California banker that institute trustee, that "the solution lies in making the opportunities here too attractive to be denied. His [Millikan's] interest in growing but he realized what a heavy job we face in trying to finance the Institute."[72]

The clincher, as Hale saw it, was to create a high-voltage laboratory associated with the physics laboratory. It was to be donated by the Southern California Edison Company, of which Robinson was a director. "This is the Edison scheme," Hale wrote. "I believe the company would get its money back in the form of new information regarding insulation and other problems connected with high voltage lines not to speak of the advertising value ... and Millikan would also have the advantage of using enormous voltage to bust up some of his atoms. This possibility which no other laboratory could match is what excites him.... When a man gets on the trial of the philosopher's stone, even if he isn't after gold you can accomplish a great deal by offering it to him."[73]

Millikan was indeed "on the trail of the philosopher's stone." In 1921–23 he was keenly interested in the problem of the "evolution" of the elements from their basic components, which were then believed to be protons and negative electrons. Stimulated by Ernest Rutherford's work on artificial transmutations, Millikan hoped to probe the secrets of the atom and its nucleus by high-voltage discharges. The High Voltage Laboratory supplied by the Southern California Edison Company was to house a million-volt transformer to assist in atomic and nuclear research. With the aid of institute trustees and Edison directors Arthur Fleming and Henry Robinson, the laboratory was built, and Hale's package, assembled to attract Millikan to Pasadena as president upon Scherer's retirement, was completed.

Millikan wrote Chicago trustee Martin Ryerson on February 8, 1921, the details of Caltech's offer: three-quarters time free for research, $50,000 a year for physics research alone, and a salary set at a grand (for the time) $15,000. Millikan proposed to Ryerson the following conditions for Chicago: $10,000 a year for ten years for equipment, $10,000 a year for ten years for research fellowships, $5,000 a year for shop facilities, and $3,000 a year for visiting Europeans. President Judson replied that he could not possibly meet the three-quarters research time that Caltech had offered and could not pledge the sums requested, but could possibly supply $10,000 for equipment for next year.[74] The situation came to a head in mid-May. Millikan, in an unusual stance, chose to play Hamlet. He did not want to leave Chicago, yet strongly felt the lure of Hale's scientific utopia. He proposed a compromise plan, the gist of which was that Millikan would divide his time equally between Chicago and Caltech, serving as director of physical research at both places. Hale was unhappy. He wrote to his wife, Evelina: "Unless he identifies himself wholly with C.I.T. and takes the presidency, I fear the enormous psychological value of acting will be lost, and with it the possibility of developing the Institute into the leading center of physics and chemistry in the country.... I am doing some tall scheming and already have some new ideas that may lead somewhere."[75]

Millikan reported to Greta:

> Hale is making himself sick over the situation.... My combination scheme Hale accepts as a last resort, but he will be terribly disappointed if I don't take the presidency.... Hale had yesterday about settled down to the compromise plan, but tonight he sees only the complete acceptance of the old Pasadena plan which you see now means throwing down a fine offer from Chicago. I wish I could split myself up into parts. This is worse torture than courted damsels ever go through for I could be perfectly happy with both suitors or with either of them.[76]

Millikan's decision would affect not only Caltech and Chicago; the proposal that he move across half a continent became an issue within the national scientific establishment. Hale told his wife that Dr. William Welch and Dr. Simon Flexner "are strongly against Millikan's acceptance of the presidency and Welch says the University of Chicago will undoubtedly meet all his demands.... Both Pupin and Dunn strongly urged Millikan to accept our offer whatever Chicago may do."[77]

Like Hale, President Judson was cool to the combination plan. "It is not practicable," he wrote to Millikan, "for a Professor to hold a permanent position in two separate institutions simultaneously."[78] Chicago's offer was much below Caltech's in the end, and the issue was settled.[79] Millikan accepted Caltech's offer on June 2, 1921, and assumed the chairmanship of the Executive Council (the presidency) and the directorship of the Norman Bridge Laboratory.

By the fall of 1921 Hale's team was assembled. Hale, Millikan, and Noyes were all influential members of the National Research Council; Millikan was already being talked of for a Nobel prize; and the Mount Wilson Observatory was one of the most famous in the world.

The triumvirate realized their dream of cooperative research in physics, chemistry, and astronomy, but lacked sufficient financing. They were in a strategic position by 1921 to make use of the network of relations they had established during the previous two decades. Their funding was "private" money; it came from the large foundations, from local (Los Angeles and Pasadena) wealth, and from private industry. Their decision to seek private rather than public funds was tactically sound and consonant with their ideological positions. Millikan wrote: "One of the most dangerous tendencies which confronts America today is the apparently growing tendency of her people to get into the habit of calling upon the state to meet all their wants. The genius of the Anglo-Saxon race has in the past lain in the development of individual initiative."[80]

By relying on "individual initiative," Millikan and Hale intended to shield their work from meddling congressmen and other representatives of the people. Hale liked to keep the threads of policy firmly in the grasp of a "group of very strong men," preferably men of his own choosing. The funding of the National Research Council and Caltech followed a similar pattern. James McKeen Cattell was correct when he wrote to Hale in 1920 that "you believe that aristocracy and patronage are favorable to science."[81]

Hale's strategic role during the war as chairman of the National Research Council and Millikan's as his vice-chairman and director of research enhanced Caltech's position in the postwar period. The National Research Council had considered itself responsible for fostering cooperation in research and stimulating both pure and applied science. Both during and after the war it forged links with major corporations and private foundations. Its advisory committee included such wealthy men as Theodore Vail, George Eastman, Pierre Du Pont, Elbert H. Gary, Cleveland E. Dodge, Andrew W. Mellon, and Elihu Root. The National Research Council had applied for and received large grants from the Carnegie and Rockefeller foundations.[82] As a clearinghouse for information it commanded an overall view of research and funding. Through the NRC Hale and Millikan extended their network of connections. As patriotic officials during the war, they found all doors open to them, and none was closed after the end of the war.

Hale's closest links were with Carnegie money. As the successful director of Mount Wilson Observatory, one of the

Carnegie Institution's most famous enterprises, he had immediate access to and influence with the highest councils. Woodward, the president of the Carnegie Institution, was a friend of Hale and of Millikan, too; as Millikan's former teacher, Woodward was lavish with praise for him.[83] When Woodward retired, Hale was seen as his natural successor. Hale refused the position and nominated instead his good friend and National Research Council associate John C. Merriam, who was named to the post.[84] Charles Walcott, Hale's friend and colleague at the National Academy of Sciences and at the National Research Council, was important in the Carnegie Institution. On the board of trustees of the Carnegie Institution during the 1920s were such NRC figures as J. J. Carty, Herbert Hoover, Elihu Root, William Welch, and Simon Flexner. Millikan, Noyes, and Hale had already received research funds from and served as advisers to the Carnegie Institution.

Hale found the Carnegie Corporation of New York another inviting source of funds. Its president in 1920 was James R. Angell, who had been chairman of the National Research Council in 1919 and who was closely tied to Hale's plans. The trustees of the Carnegie Corporation included Merriam, Carty, and Root, who was Hale's friend and adviser. Access to consideration for funds from the Rockefeller Foundation was ensured by the important positions in it held by Flexner and by Vernon Kellogg, the NRC's permanent secretary. Cattell's observation went to the heart of the matter: "Whether the Research Council belongs to the National Academy, or the National Academy belongs to the Research Council, or both are satellites of Pasadena is a problem of three bodies that is difficult of solution. The Carnegie Corporation, the Rockefeller Foundation and the National Research Council are another problem of three bodies."[85]

More important for Caltech's immediate future was Hale's entrée, through Throop's board of trustees, to the wealthiest circles in and around Los Angeles. The appeals that Hale and Millikan made in the 1920s were based on their belief in the destiny and future glory of Southern California. Hale had revealed the main outlines of this appeal as early as 1912 in a letter to his friend and Throop trustee Charles F. Holder:

In the development of electrical engineering, especially long distance power transmission; in the great extent and output of the California oil fields which require the most thorough scientific study for their proper development; in the extensive hydraulic undertakings, such as the great aqueduct now being built to supply Los Angeles and the surrounding region with water; in the shipbuilding and other industries which will be so affected by the opening of the Panama Canal; in the rapid growth of Los Angeles and other cities of Southern California which involves a demand for many skilled engineers; in fact in all of the activities which accompany the extraordinary rapid flow of population into this section of the United States, a first class institute of technology like Throop can accomplish much more here than elsewhere.[86]

The argument was simply that as the Los Angeles region continued to expand, it would require experts in research, development, and management. An institute such as Throop and, later, Caltech was promoted as a reservoir of scientific experts for modern regional development.

Hale's themes were advanced during the 1920s by Millikan, who claimed that "here in Southern California the eyes of the United States are focused upon you as they are upon no other region in the United States."[87] Later he assured a receptive audience that the world's biggest industrial problem was the transmission of energy, and that the biggest problem of the future would be the direct use of the sun's energy. He said that California had already contributed to the solution of the first problem, and, owing to its geographical position and "the character of the race that inhabits it," it might be expected to contribute to the solution of the latter. He continued:

Southern California will then inevitably develop in the near future.... That development can only take place effectively around the great centers of research and specialized study which have already been created in the Mount Wilson Observatory, the California Institute of Technology, and the Huntington Library.... The present rapid growth of Southern California, the influx into it of a population which is twice as largely Anglo-Saxon as that existing in New York ... the preceding establishment of the Mount Wilson Observatory, the Huntington Library and the California Institute, geographic and climatic conditions all combine to make this a time and this a place of exceptional opportunity.[88]

Millikan boasted that "California marks now as England did three centuries ago the farthest western outpost of Arian civilization."[89]

It is instructive to list some of the local people who infused money into Caltech during the 1920s: Henry M. Robinson, banker, director of Southern California Edison Company, with interests in lumber, copper and real estate; Norman Bridge; William Kerckhoff, hydroelectric tycoon and lumber magnate; R. R. Blacker, lumber magnate; R. C. Gillis, real estate developer; C. W. Gates, lumber operator; and above all, Arthur Fleming, president of the board of trustees. Fleming was a lumber magnate whose broad financial interests involved railroads, mining, and real estate. By the time Millikan arrived in Pasadena, Fleming had already been a large donor, and to ensure Millikan's coming he had pledged his entire fortune, apart from an annuity to be set aside for him, for Caltech's endowment. The sum he turned over to Caltech was estimated at more than $4.2 million. The list could be extended, but already the essential point emerges clearly: donors were involved in those key areas of finance and industry that would benefit from and at the same time ensure Los Angeles' rapid growth: power, water, real estate, banking, and building materials. If Hale and Millikan were right, Caltech could provide the scientific and technical manpower for regional growth.

Caltech did participate in numerous efforts in applied science that directly repaid some of the local businessmen who supported it. It helped the Southern California Edison Company complete in 1923 the long line from Big Creek to Los Angeles, carrying an unprecedented 220,000 volts. The Caltech wind tunnel and school of aeronautics contributed to the development of the DC-3 by Douglas Aviation. The Colorado River aqueduct project in the early 1930s employed Caltech geologists and civil, mechanical, and electrical engineers. Romeo Martel's seismographic laboratory aided in the planning of earthquake-resistant buildings. Noyes's chemical laboratory contributed to the synthesis of insulin. C. C. Lauritsen's high-voltage X-ray tube was employed in the treatment of cancer.

The California promoters of Caltech were not primarily interested in short-term personal profit, however. Hale and, later, Millikan appealed rather to their sense of destiny. California embodied for them, as for many others, modern America—a raw land to be developed by science, technology, and business into Western civilization's greatest triumph. Their past efforts, aside from bringing them tremendous fortunes, had made the Los Angeles area thrive. By supporting Caltech, they would continue—Hale and Millikan promised them—to play an essential role in regional development.

Local money provided the base from which Millikan and Hale sought additional support for Caltech. It ensured a sound institution that could in turn attract further money for research. Hale turned to the large foundations for money for physics and chemistry and, receiving it, transformed the nature of Caltech.

As director of the Mount Wilson Observatory, Hale planned to bring to Pasadena leaders in physics and chemistry to work with his astrophysicists to create a world center for research. He later wrote, "I easily foresaw that [Caltech's] departments of physics, chemistry and mathematics would meet just such requirements as the Mount Wilson Observatory greatly needed but could not supply from his own funds.[90] By 1921 Mount Wilson was a highly regarded research center in astronomy and astrophysics. Its policy—to develop and apply methods of physics and chemistry—was successful. The 100-inch reflecting telescope it acquired in 1917 opened new research avenues. Its improved light-gathering power enabled Michelson, a research associate, to separate and measure unresolved double stars by interferometer methods. It enabled Harlow Shapley to photograph hundreds of millions of new stars. Charles G. Abbot, another research associate, used the telescope to determine the spectral energy curves of bright stars and to measure the radiation of faint ones. Edwin Hubble studied the polarization of light from nebulas. J. C. Kapteyn worked in theoretical astrophysics in connection with the motion and arrangement of stellar systems. Henry Norris Russell worked on the astrophysical theory of ionization in stellar atmospheres.[91]

The permanent staff at Mount Wilson, in addition to Hale, included Walter S. Adams, who worked in stellar spectroscopy; Arthur S. King, who supervised the physical laboratory; Charles

St. John, who examined solar rotation; and Adriaan van Maanen, who examined parallaxes. The physical laboratory, which implemented the observatory's policy of interpreting celestial phenomena by laboratory experiments, installed a powerful electromagnet to apply researches on the Zeeman effect to anomalies in the magnetic phenomena of sunspots. The laboratory also had equipment for studying the effect of large electric fields on spectra. "We have not," Hale insisted, "adhered narrowly to the viewpoint of the astronomer, but have attacked our problems with the general interests of research in mind, without endeavoring to draw any boundary line between astronomy and physics."[92]

By 1921 Noyes, as director of the Gates Laboratory, was well along in his efforts to build a first-rate center for chemical research. Two promising young workers in the laboratory were James H. Ellis, a research associate in physical chemistry, and Roscoe Dickinson, a National Research Fellow who in 1920 had received one of Caltech's first Ph.Ds. When Noyes came to Pasadena on a full-time basis early in 1920 he brought with him Ralph Wyckoff. Within a couple of years Richard Bozorth and Linus Pauling joined them, and Caltech quickly established a reputation for leadership in the field of X-ray crystallography. The Gates Laboratory was moved by the spirit of cooperative research; it was a place not "for the individualist in science or research," Noyes wrote, "but for men who are interested in cooperating with one another.[93]

Millikan's first priority upon arriving in Pasadena was to build an important physics program. He recalled later that Noyes and Hale were strongly behind him in this matter; they believed that if physics were to succeed, the other sciences would, too, for physics was the underpinning of the other disciplines.[94] Millikan found several good people already at Caltech: Harry Bateman, who worked in mathematics and aeronautics; E. C. Watson, who had been an assistant at Chicago; and W. T. Whitney, who was an assistant in physics and likewise had been at Chicago. Millikan brought with him Ira Bowen as his assistant.

In May 1921 a plan was drafted—largely by Hale—for an Institute of Physics and Chemistry in Pasadena. Caltech hoped to obtain support from the Rockefeller Foundation, but after Simon Flexner saw Rockefeller in mid-May the plan fell through.[95] The plan emphasized the need for large funds for research in physics and chemistry. It argued that the interdependence of chemistry and physics required sophisticated (and expensive) equipment. Currently attainable laboratory conditions must be supplemented by "transcendental" temperatures, electric and magnetic fields, gravitational fields and ionization conditions attainable only in the sun and stars. Proximity to the Mount Wilson Observatory was therefore not merely desirable but absolutely necessary. Physics and chemistry "are so closely intertwined that the investigation of their fundamental laws should be undertaken by a single research organization comprising departments of physics and chemistry working in the most intimate cooperation." The California Institute of Technology, it was suggested, would seem an appropriate place. The cooperative research carried out in the Gates and Bridge Laboratories and at Mount Wilson would serve national needs by training scientific personnel: "By utilizing graduate students and fellows as the main research body of the Institute, working under the guidance of a few investigators of the highest type, the great purpose, now so urgent as a national need, of training research men for the universities and industries while turning out new discoveries in physics and chemistry can be accomplished.... Another advantage of this plan ... is that the cost of research is greatly reduced by utilizing a large staff of teaching fellows while its quality is amply demonstrated by the results.[96]

When prospects for Rockefeller support dimmed, Hale took the Caltech plan immediately to the Carnegie Corporation. On May 26, 1921, he met with the corporation's president, James R. Angell, a friend and close NRC associate. Hale recorded the outcome of the meeting in his diary: if Millikan were to accept Caltech's offer, "Angell thinks M. could count in reasonable time on very substantial assistance from C.C. which Angell could recommend. If he were continuing as Pres. he would guarantee favorable action." Hale also met with Pritchett, who was soon to be acting president of the corporation and who was "strongly in favor"; Pritchett called the plan a "perfectly corking thing to do." Root, a Carnegie trustee and NRC associate, called it a "fascinating scheme."[97]

Assured of favorable and friendly consideration, Hale drafted a preliminary proposal as soon as Millikan's plans were set. On June 4 Hale wrote to Angell giving details of a coordinated research plan for the study of "the constitution of matter and its relation to the phenomena of radiation." Further advance in this field, he wrote, was to be expected "largely through the utilization of the most powerful agencies, such as enormously high temperatures and pressures, high-voltage discharges, and intense magnetic fields, combined with the most refined methods of measurement." Moreover, the proximity of the California Institute to the Mount Wilson Observatory promised fruitful exploitation of the "scores of experiments [that] are being performed before our very eyes in . . . celestial laboratories." He concluded that "the physicist and the chemist may profit greatly by cooperation with the astrophysicist."[98]

The proposal to the Carnegie Corporation is a succinct statement of Hale's latest ideas on cooperative research. Recent events in physics and astrophysics had validated his commitment to the cooperative ideal. Earlier he had concentrated on the interactions between astrophysics and experimental physics and chemistry. Since then Niels Bohr's theory of the atom and Arnold Sommerfeld's relativistic interpretation of the fine structure of atomic spectra made spectroscopy central to theoretical physics and astrophysics. Millikan and Noyes as well as Hale were convinced that quantum theoretical physics placed heavy new demands on the experimental and observational sciences. A revolution in scientific instrumentation would be required to unravel the mysteries of atomic and stellar interiors. Hale wrote to Angell: "It is therefore important that the investigations be undertaken with the aid of ample financial resources. . . . It is also important that the problem be studied with the close cooperation of able physicists, astrophysicists, mathematicians and chemists."[99]

In the fall of 1921, Millikan, Hale, and Noyes drafted a large and impressive grant proposal to the Carnegie Corporation of New York, urging support for a joint attack on the problems of radiation and matter; the work was to be carried out by

A. A. Noyes, G. E. Hale, and R. A. Millikan. Courtesy of the Archives, California Institute of Technology.

Millikan's Norman Bridge Laboratory, Noyes's Gates Laboratory, and Hale's Mount Wilson Observatory. On September 17, 1921, the board of trustees of Caltech transmitted the proposal to the Carnegie Corporation. The proposal requested $40,000 annually for partial maintenance of the project and a one-time grant of $500,000 as endowment. The Carnegie Corporation granted up to $30,000 annually, but postponed a decision on the endowment.

The September 1921 grant proposal was more detailed and elaborate than earlier proposals, but its argument was substantially the same as before. Although the proposed research was to be undertaken purely for scientific purposes, the high-voltage work planned by the physics laboratory was related to "probably the most important *commercial* problem of the next half-century, i.e. the transmission of energy ... to distant centers of population or to distant agricultural areas ... through new developments in high voltage transmission." The proposal argued in the now familiar way that in an era when the nuclear atom was central to an understanding of the constitution of matter, the problems of astronomy, physics, and chemistry converged. "The present plan is to create a *single center* equipped with powerful facilities for attacking the problem as a whole from the standpoint of all these sister sciences." Southern California's benign weather, the transparency of its atmosphere (for telescopic studies), and its proximity to mountains and ocean (for electromagnetic marine signaling) combined to favor research in the physical sciences. The work of the physicist and chemist "and that of the Mount Wilson observers mutually support and interpret one another."[100] Indeed, the heart of the proposal was an appeal for cooperative research:

> The physicist, who approaches the complex problem by the simplest and most direct route, deals only with the chemical elements, and evolves powerful methods of research which enable him to penetrate to the core of the atom, to visualize the electrons swinging in their orbits, and to remove them one by one for detailed study. The chemist, concerned primarily with the union of the atoms into molecules, and the combinations of molecules of one or more elements, necessarily attacks matter of greater complexity, extending all the way from the single atom of hydrogen to compounds

containing hundreds of linked atoms of many kinds. The astrophysicist, permitted by his powerful telescopes to penetrate to the depths of the universe, observes matter in the state of luminous gaseous elements, associated in the cooler stars with certain chemical compounds. The cosmic crucibles in this vast laboratory of nature exhibit conditions of temperature and pressure often transcending those attainable in the laboratory, and thus present for observation experiments on an immense scale, the interpretation of which has already added much to our knowledge of physics and chemistry.

Any general attack upon the constitution of matter must therefore approach the problem simultaneously along the three converging lines of physics, chemistry, and astrophysics.

The progress of research, especially during the last quarter century, has brought us to the present critical juncture, when the possibilities of such a joint attack have reached an extraordinarily favorable state. In each of the branches of science involved, the methods and instruments of research have advanced to a very high degree of development. Discovery has followed discovery, now in one subject, now in another, each throwing new and increasing illumination into the other fields. The application of the spectroscope of astronomy, affording the means of determining the chemical composition, distances, motions, temperatures, pressures and magnetic state of the stars, has led to many advances to fundamental importance to chemistry and physics. The rise of physical chemistry, which transformed chemistry from a largely descriptive to an exact science and revealed the fundamental role played by electrically charged particles in solution, opened another world of new thought. The extraordinary discoveries and developments in physics, particularly in the fields of radioactivity, the electrical nature of matter, X-rays and radiation, have brought to light wholly unexpected relationships between the elements which are of the greatest significance, both from the purely scientific and practical point of view.[101]

Millikan was responsible for carrying out the program outlined in the Carnegie proposal. "My first job at C.I.T.," he recalled, "was the development of a program in physics," for physics, together with chemistry, was the "basis of all engineering and biology."[102] He had the advantage that Caltech, unlike other universities, was not encumbered with many people and programs that were behind the times; it had only a few such people. Thus he was able to staff the Physics Department to his own specifications. Of the full professors already there, only Harry Bateman was an asset to Millikan. A graduate of Cambridge and Johns Hopkins universities, Bateman had been appointed in 1917; he represented strength in mathematical physics, a specialty that Millikan was keen to develop. The other professor of physics was Lucien Gilmore, who had received his A.B. from Stanford in 1894; he was a member of the old Throop faculty and took little part in the research plans for Caltech.

One of Millikan's first steps was to invite illustrious physicists to Caltech to ensure international attention. Michelson came as research associate in 1920 and Lorentz in 1921–22 and 1922–23. Charles Galton Darwin came as visiting professor in 1922–23. Other research associates included Paul Ehrenfest in 1923, C. V. Raman in 1924, Vilhelm Bjerknes in 1924, and Arnold Sommerfeld in 1928. Two permanent appointments that greatly strengthened theoretical physics at Caltech were those of Paul Epstein in 1921 and Richard Tolman in 1922. Epstein was educated at Moscow under P. N. Lebedev and later worked under Sommerfeld in Munich. He was a gifted theoretical physicist and was later charged with teaching the advanced courses in theoretical and mathematical physics.[103]

Epstein was not Millikan's first choice; he considered Darwin, Max Mason, and Peter Debye as well.[104] Only when Darwin proved reluctant to come to California on a permanent basis did Millikan move to hire Epstein. There were problems with the Epstein appointment that were extraprofessional. Millikan wrote to Hale in July 1921, "I am still hesitating about Epstein but will certainly write him at once if Darwin can't come. Do you think we might want to get Epstein anyway even though a Jew?" He did in the end hire Epstein "even though a Jew," but failed to fill another need, that of a first-rate electrical engineer, owing to suspicions concerning the Jewishness of the candidate. "If [Leonard F.] Fuller is coming with us you might show him the enclosed in re Tyksciker [Joseph T. Tykosciner]. But alas another Jew!! . . . . His knowledge of Westinghouse processes would be of the greatest value. But we can't get more than about one Jew anyway!"[105] Tykosciner was not hired, and left Westinghouse for the University of Illinois, where he helped to found one of America's greatest departments of electrical engineering.[106]

But able scientists such as Richard Tolman soon joined Epstein. A graduate of M.I.T., Tolman had known Noyes during his years as graduate student and research associate there. Before coming to Caltech in 1922 he was professor of chemistry at the University of Illinois and director of the Fixed Nitrogen Laboratory of the Department of Agriculture. He was appointed professor of physical chemistry and mathematical physics at Caltech.[107] Tolman was "a man of great originality and rather unusual general ability," according to Noyes, who had proposed him for a post at Throop as early as 1911.[108] In 1921 Noyes was convinced that Tolman's work was "among the most important lines of research in physical chemistry that I know of today. I have especially in mind the problems on the rate of reaction, on the effect of electrical discharges on chemical reactions in bases, and on the theory of catalysis from the adsorption standpoint."[109] J. Robert Oppenheimer joined the faculty in 1928, dividing his time between Pasadena and Berkeley.

By the end of the 1920s the scientific talent at Caltech was impressive. According to its 1930 *Bulletin,* the Caltech faculty included Thomas Hunt Morgan, Theodor von Karman, A. H. Sturtevant, Linus Pauling, Theodosius Dobzhansky, Carl Anderson, and Fritz Zwicky. A notable addition that year was Albert Einstein, who came as a research associate.[110]

From the beginning, Millikan's tactics yielded remarkable success. Pasadena quickly became a center for activity in the physical sciences, and the cooperative ideal appeared to be working well in practice. The staffs of Caltech and the observatory interacted closely; in 1921–22, for example, both staffs attended the lectures of Lorentz and Epstein, and they established an Astronomy and Physics Club that met weekly to discuss work of common interest. Noyes worked closely with the physicists associated with the observatory on the theory of ionization and they initiated a joint seismological program.[111] The visitors were used as resources; Ehrenfest wrote joint papers with Epstein, Bateman, and Tolman.[112] Ira Sprague Bowen, Millikan's assistant, increasingly associated himself with the interests of the observatory, and ultimately became its director.[113]

Judged strictly by quantity of research, Caltech's performance was excellent. A survey of three prestigious journals—*Physical Review, Proceedings of the National Academy of Sciences,* and *Astrophysical Journal*—reveals that of the 435 papers they published during 1925 and 1926, Caltech scientists accounted for 66; Harvard followed with 59, Chicago with 39, Princeton with 34, Mount Wilson Observatory with 30, Cornell with 22, and Michigan with 18. Together Caltech and Mount Wilson accounted for more than a fourth of the contributions from scientists at major institutions and for over a fifth of the contributions from scientists at all institutions.[114] Karl Compton made a survey in 1927 that revealed that the number of major physics publications from Caltech in 1927 was 50; the next most productive institution accounted for only 33. In attracting productive younger scientists, Caltech far outstripped its competitors. Caltech attracted 25 national and international research fellows in physics to May 1928; Princeton followed with 18, Harvard with 16, Chicago with 14; Johns Hopkins, Yale, and Michigan had 5 each, and California had 4. By 1928 there were 14 research fellows at Caltech, accounting for nearly 10 percent of the graduate school apart from faculty.[115] The number of graduate students at Caltech grew from a handful in 1921 to more than 100 in 1926. These figures indicate the remarkable speed with which Caltech achieved prominence as a research and training center.

Millikan, as chief executive of Caltech, was keen to improve its scientific standing, and he was now able to operate from a position of strength. In 1923 he began to cast about for personnel for a new department of geology. After two years of desultory searching, and with the aid of John Merriam of the Carnegie Institution, he found just the right person, John P. Buwalda of the University of California at Berkeley. Millikan wanted a westerner, for an easterner would require substantial retraining in order to deal with the geological problems of California. In March 1925 a formal offer was tendered to Buwalda, who politely but firmly declined. Millikan began to apply the "Caltech touch"; he invited Professor and Mrs. Buwalda to Pasadena for a lovely May weekend. Within two weeks, Buwalda accepted "with great happiness" Millikan's renewed offer.[116] The money for the new department came from the Carnegie Institution of Washington and from such private donors as Allan Balch, Henry Robinson, and the family of Seeley Mudd.[117]

In 1926 Millikan wished to develop aerodynamics/aeronautics at Caltech. Already represented by Harry Bateman and A. A. Merrill, the discipline was rapidly advanced with the addition of the Guggenheim Aeronautical Laboratory, donated by the Daniel Guggenheim Fund for the Promotion of Aeronautics, and the appointment, strongly backed by Epstein, of the aerodynamicist Theodor von Karman.[118]

By 1925 Millikan was also prepared to initiate a major effort to establish a department of biological sciences. Once again he wished to build from his central core of strength, his powerful department of physics. In his application for support to the General Education Board in 1925, Millikan asserted: "It needs no demonstration that one of the most crying needs of Southern California . . . is for the spread throughout its length and breadth of saner, more scientific influences in biology and medicine than now exist here. It is however desirable to introduce as soon as possible *those branches of biology* which have close relations with physics and chemistry and of which the successful development depends on intimate relations with strong departments of physics and chemistry."[119] The appointments he would like to make, he explained, were John Jacob Abel of Johns Hopkins as professor of biochemistry and chemical pharmacology, and Archibald Vivian Hill of the University of London as professor of biophysics. These appointments were not made; instead, Thomas Hunt Morgan, the distinguished geneticist, was lured west from Columbia. Millikan reported gleefully that "Morgan is keen on the possibility of luring into his field some of the sharks in the new physics."[120] By mid-1927 Morgan had resigned from Columbia University to become head of Caltech's first biology department.[121]

As early as 1923 Millikan acclaimed Caltech a success. He believed Caltech would have a great impact on the national scene. According to Millikan, Caltech furnished "very exceptional opportunities for very exceptional men." Like Hale, he believed that the "progress of civilization is determined by the very few men of vision and capacity which each age produced." The "mainsprings of the twentieth century," Millikan claimed, "are all found in the sciences, particularly in the physical sciences." America's past success had depended on its easily accessible wealth. Its future success depended on "developing men who have the capacity to dig in deeper veins, to create new processes, to eliminate waste, to succeed under more difficult conditions and in the face of keener competition." As the westernmost outpost of "Aryan civilization," California was the region most favorably located to solve the world's future problems, "which will have to do with the relations of eastern and western races."[122] Caltech's task was to train leaders in science and industry who could meet these problems.

Millikan's argument is at base what has come to be termed "technocratic." The conviction that America's destiny is closely intertwined with the development of a corps of scientifically trained experts has become influential in the twentieth century. Millikan, among others, was convinced that advances in pure science and their applications would determine America's future. Millikan's views represented those of leading scientific circles. Caltech was unique only in the speed of its rise to prominence and in the clarity with which it espoused themes that would later become common at many institutions of higher learning in America. Pasadena's example was duly noted and emulated.

The rise of Caltech reveals important characteristics of the political economy of American science after World War I. James McKeen Cattell was correct in seeing that Hale and his allies chose the path of aristocracy and patronage. "You believe that aristocracy and patronage are favorable to science," Cattell wrote to Hale in 1920; "I believe that they must be discarded for the cruder but more rigorous ways of democracy."[123] The "patrons" were captains of industry and commerce and controllers of great fortunes, such as the Carnegie and Rockefeller foundations. Hale, Millikan, and Noyes were, in a sense, their counterparts in the world of science: they were prominent scientists who moved easily among prominent financiers and industrialists, spoke their language, and shared their assumptions about the world and its future. Scientific patronage depended on the willingness of the patron to see the importance of research, which in turn depended on the conviction that science was central to the wealth and proper functioning of a modern nation. Hale, Millikan, and Noyes were reinforced in their conviction by their friend Herbert Hoover. Hoover was one of Hale's early choices for the National Research Council, and his career as secretary of commerce testified to his dedication to the advancement of pure and applied science. In an address on science and the nation in 1927 Hoover maintained: "The more one observes, the more clearly does he see that it is in the soil of pure science that are found the origins of all our modern industry and commerce. In fact our civilization and our large population are wholly builded upon our scientific discoveries. It is the increased productivity of men which have [sic] come from these discoveries that has defeated the prophecies of Malthus."[124]

Scientific patronage worked through the tight network of personal relationships that Hale had nourished over several decades and that centered on the National Research Council. The NRC collected information on the promotion of research and administered funds appropriated by foundations, industrial concerns, and individuals. It functioned smoothly and with little criticism. In general, funds were distributed fairly among leading institutions. If Caltech was a large beneficiary, few outsiders doubted its capacity to use resources in the best interests of science. The first setback to this patronage network occurred in the late 1920s, when Hale attempted to collect $20 million for research from private industry. The National Research Fund, headed by Hoover and later by Carty and by Frank B. Jewett, president of the Bell Telephone Laboratories, failed. The NRC group that planned it had miscalculated private industry's willingness to support pure research; the fund collapsed in 1934, having accomplished nothing.[125] During the Great Depression and World War II, private sources were neither willing nor able to meet the vast new demands of scientific research. The federal government eventually assumed the responsibilities that Hale, Noyes, and Millikan had tried to keep in the private sphere. Access to the public purse replaced the elaborate system that Hale and his allies had painstakingly built.

5

The Scientist as Sage

Hurrah! Hurrah! the waters o'er
 The mountain's steep decline,
Time, space, have yielded to my power,
 The world, the world is mine.
 —*McGuffey's Reader*

When Robert Millikan was demobilized after World War I, he faced a difficult but sweet career decision. He had to determine the future course of his research, and he was obliged to face the implications of his new, elevated status in the profession. Few prior commitments weighed upon him. At that moment he possessed the freedom we all seek but over which those who have it agonize.

Even during his most active periods of entrepreneurial and administrative activity, he managed to invest many hours in physics research and to inaugurate new investigative programs that were to turn out to be exceedingly fruitful.[1] Upon his discharge from war service in January 1919, Millikan returned to Chicago to develop a research program that he had begun before the war. But he approached his work from a new vantage point, and outwardly at least with increased confidence. Some colleagues and students recalled incipient hubris: Michelson's daughter reported that "Millikan's pride rose understandably with each new honor" and that Michelson liked to share "the latest 'Millikanism' with his wife at dinner table."[2] Vern O. Knudsen, who was a student at Chicago during the late teens, remembered that "Millikan was an egotistic person, very much," and that he "was very much concerned about his own reputation." Colleague Henry Gale is reported to have exclaimed: "Goddamn that Robert Millikan. He's so goddamned selfish, and he doesn't know that he's so goddamned selfish." But Knudsen also recalled that by 1917 "everybody thought he'd win the Nobel."[3] It quickly became clear that the importance of his new series of investigations would have to mirror his elevated status in the profession. The expectations of peers are in themselves strong pressures.

His previous successful researches had aimed at the heart of new theories of matter and radiation: the nature of the electron and the character of light. He wished now to probe inside the atom, in order to determine precisely the map of the atom's interior and if possible gain some further insight into what had always pricked his imagination, the evolution and transformations of the elements.

The decade before Millikan's arrival to Pasadena had been one of the most exciting and fruitful in the history of physics. The plethora of data and speculation opened by the exploitation of the spectroscope, by the discovery of X rays, and by investigations into radioactivity were beginning to come under some reasonable control. Ernest Rutherford's nuclear atom and the physics of the quantum were joined in Niels Bohr's landmark atomic model. Bohr's atom was a spectroscopic one: it was designed to cope with the enormous quantity of line-spectra data that physicists had long suspected would yield information about atomic structure.[4] Millikan later remarked that when "it was devised, spectroscopy was a veritable dark continent in physics. With the aid of the Bohr atom the dark continent in physics has become the best explored and best understood, the most civilized portion of the world of physics. It has been an exciting game of exploration."[5]

The "exciting game" was further stimulated by the discoveries of Henry G. J. Moseley, the British physicist, later killed in World War I. Moseley, working along lines first laid out by the X-ray crystallographers Max von Laue and the Braggs, William Henry and (William) Lawrence, accurately determined the frequencies of the X rays characteristic of the elements. Moseley showed that the square roots of these frequencies are related in a simple way. They constitute a simple arithmetic progression: each member of the series is obtained from the previous member when the same quantity is added. Moseley saw at once that his formulas could be used to test the periodic table, for his series of X-ray frequencies (with a few exceptions) follows the chemists' series of atomic weights.[6] Furthermore, research on radioactivity produced evidence that when a substance loses a doubly charged positive particle (an alpha), it moves two places to the left in the periodic table, and when it loses a single negative particle, it moves one place to the right. The chemical nature of a substance depends, therefore, on its atomic number, or the number of positive charges in its nucleus. The periodic table could now be reconstructed along physical lines, on the basis of this notion of atomic number. "There is in the atom," Moseley stated, "a fundamental quantity which...increases by regular steps...from one element to the next. This quantity can only be the charge on the central positive nucleus."[7]

It was Millikan's intention to follow along the path pioneered by Moseley. He signaled his intentions in his presidential address before the Physical Society in December 1916. The address, titled "Radiation and Atomic Structure," sketches his strategy. "It has been chiefly the facts of radiation which have provided reliable information about the inner structure of the atom itself." Charles Glover Barkla, Rutherford, and above all Moseley had furnished evidence concerning the "electronic" and nuclear constituents of the atom: "In a research which is destined to rank as one of the dozen most brilliant in conception, skillful in execution, and illuminating in results in the history of science, a young man but twenty-six years old [Moseley] threw open the windows through which we can now glimpse the sub-atomic world with a definiteness and certainty never dreamed of before." The task before the physics community was articulation of the atomic model of Niels Bohr:

> If then the test of truth in a physical theory is large success both in the prediction of new relationships and in correctly and exactly accounting for old ones, the theory of non-radiating orbits is one of the well-established truths of modern physics. For the present at least it is truth and no other theory of atomic structure can be considered until it has shown itself able to approach it in fertility. I know of no competitor which is as yet in sight.

Unmodified, however, the Bohr theory applies only to hydrogen and helium; for heavier elements, "the radiations give us no information about conditions or behaviors of the external electrons which have to do with the phenomena of valency."[8]

The new program would deal directly with the questions of atomic structure, investigated through spectroscopic studies, and would later be joined by studies of the "evolution" of the elements, examined through investigations of penetrating radiation, or, as they were later known, "cosmic rays." His plan was described in the joint grant proposal to the Carnegie Corporation in 1921, in which Millikan (along with Hale and Noyes) wrote:

> Matter occurs in nature under the widest variety of composition and form. The physicist, who approaches the complex problem by the simplest and most direct route, deals only with the chemical elements, and evolves powerful methods of research which enable him to penetrate to the core of the atom, to visualize the electrons swinging in their orbits, and to remove them one by one for detailed study.[9]

The first major step in the new program was the development of a new technique. As early as 1905 Millikan had been working on problems related to sparking potentials in vacuums,[10] and had found that the spark discharge of a condenser, emitting ultraviolet light, could be maintained under high potentials in a vacuum. According to Millikan, it occurred to him that such discharges, labeled "hot spark discharges," could solve a troublesome spectroscopic problem. One difficulty in the mapping of the spectrum of extreme ultraviolet light emitted from atoms was the high absorption of very short wavelength radiations by the fluorite window and prism spectroscopic equipment then in general use.[11] Millikan believed he could circumvent these difficulties by using a vacuum spectrometer employing high vacuums, hot sparks, and a concave reflecting grating. In a series of papers with R. A. Sawyer and Ira Bowen, Millikan was able to make a considerable extension of the map of the ultraviolet spectrum; they had been able to photograph, measure the wavelength, and analyze the atoms of light elements and multiply ionized atoms of the heavier atoms. They found about 1,000 new lines, and showed that their wavelengths were consistent with the Bohr theory.[12] Millikan and Bowen established the essential unity of the optical and X-ray spectra, demonstrating, in Millikan's words, that "optical spectra are quite like x-ray spectra in that large gaps occur between frequencies due to electrons in successive rings or shells."[13] Millikan also worked with his graduate students on the emission of electrons from cold metal surfaces from points at which the field gradient is large. Millikan and B. E. Shackelford concluded in 1920 that their "experiments indicate that the discharge is conditioned by surface impurities and cast doubt upon the conclusion that there is a particular field strength at which electrons begin to be pulled out of a pure metal."[14] Carl Eyring, then a Caltech graduate student, and Millikan found in 1926 that the *field current* (a term they apparently introduced) depended on the local field gradient at the point of emission and not on the total potential difference along the wire. Furthermore, its behavior was incompatible with the assumption that it was a thermionic current in a strong electrical field.[15] The quantum mechanical explanation for the phenomenon was given by J. Robert Oppenheimer and by R. H. Fowler and Lothar Nordheim, who independently explained field current as leakage through a potential barrier.[16]

The third segment of the program dealt with what was usually termed at the time "the penetrating radiation" and was to become known by Millikan's name for it, cosmic rays. At the beginning of the century several researchers found that normal laboratory air was slightly ionized.[17] Shortly thereafter, Ernest Rutherford and H. L. Cooke, and also John McLennan and Eli Burton, both teams working in Canada, demonstrated a marked reduction in ionization when the detecting vessel is shielded by lead or some other absorbing material, indicating that the ionization arises from some outside radiation that was able to penetrate thin metal walls.[18] It was supposed for a long time afterward that the ionization was caused by radiation from small amounts of radioactive material in rocks and soil. In 1909 Karl Kurz reviewed all the evidence and concluded that none of it contradicted the hypothesis that the penetrating radiation was caused by such radioactive impurities in the earth's crust.[19]

A contingent hypothesis, that radiation ought to decrease at high altitudes, was tested atop high towers and by daring balloon ascents by Karl Bergwitz and Albert Gockel, accounts of which were published in 1910 and 1911.[20] The results were uncertain, but Gockel uncovered a strange anomaly: at 4,500 meters, the intensity of the ionization was actually *greater* than at the earth's surface. Victor Hess and (independently) Werner Kolhörster mounted numerous balloon ascents and improved the apparatus. They were able to show that above 2,000 meters the penetrating radiation increases and above 3,000 meters there is a marked rise in intensity.[21] Hess and Kolhörster were able to attain heights of 5,200 and 9,000 meters respectively. Hess suggested that there is a very penetrating radiation that enters the atmosphere from above, the first glimmer of what were to be known as cosmic rays. But the nature of this radiation, its absorption properties, and even its existence were matters of great uncertainty in the decade following Hess's suggestion.

Millikan became interested in the penetrating radiation shortly before America's involvement in World War I. His concern is not surprising; he had long been interested in radioactivity, and the research programs that dealt with the penetrating radiation had been conceded to be a part of the study of radioactive phenomena. Hess and his co-worker M. Kofler insisted, however, that the rays came from outside the atmosphere; they still believed them to be radium and thorium emanations.[22] When Millikan was released from the army, he resolved to return to the questions raised by Hess and the others. In a letter to Robert Woodward of the Carnegie Institution of Washington dated May 6, 1919, Millikan requested assistance for a project of research "upon the penetrating radiation and the degree of ionization existing in the regions of the atmosphere between elevations of five miles and twenty miles." He proposed to carry out his investigations "by designing and sending up in sounding balloons self-recording instruments of a new type." By innovating apparatus—the use of unmanned flight and self-recording instrumentation—Millikan would have been able once again to bring clarity and precision to a scientific problem area. "We have already indications of a penetrating radiation which has its source outside the earth," he wrote. "If such a source does exist it is a matter of extraordinary importance to have it revealed and studied. I know of no way other than that suggested in which definite knowledge as to the existence or non-existence of such a source can be obtained."[23] It seems clear that Millikan saw his problem as first to demonstrate what had merely been indicated, that existence of the extra-atmospheric penetrating radiation, and second, if it existed at all, to determine its characteristics. The Carnegie Corporation grant proposal submitted in 1921 by Hale, Millikan, and Noyes confirms this view. In the section headed "The Research Program from the Standpoint of Physics," very little space is devoted to the penetrating radiation; the proposal merely states that it is Millikan's intention to "study the penetrating radiations of the upper air to determine whether these are of cosmic or of terrestrial origin."[24]

What the Carnegie proposal emphasizes is another, as yet unlinked, interest of Millikan. From his early researches of the first decade of the century, Millikan's imagination had been captured by radioactivity, the transformation of the elements, and its potential insights into the construction of matter. He was of course not alone; many physicists shared these concerns, and the provocative work of Moseley reinforced their interest.

Moseley's work revived interest in a hypothesis that had been advanced a century earlier. The chemist William Prout had argued that atomic weights were multiples of that of hydrogen, and therefore hydrogen may be taken to be the primordial element. Prout's speculation foundered on the rock of precise measurement: the multiple relationships are not exact. But twentieth-century physicists were confident of resolving all difficulties, and the assumption was widely held that the elements were built up out of hydrogen nuclei (protons) and electrons. Arnold Sommerfeld endorsed Prout in this way: "The atoms of the various elements must be similarly constructed out of identical units."[25] Millikan himself put it a bit more romantically: "It looks as if the dream of Thales of Miletus has actually come true and that we have found not only a primordial element out of which all substances are made, but that that primordial element is hydrogen itself."[26]

The exact work of Francis William Aston with the mass spectograph served only to reinforce interest in atom building. Aston's "whole number rule"—that, with the exception of hydrogen, atomic weights of the elements are whole numbers—"removes the only serious objection to a unitary theory of matter."[27] Hydrogen was measured at very slightly more than unity; the "lost" mass in the building up of heavier elements from the proton was explained away by a "packing effect" that was originally viewed as an electromagnetic contraction.[28] Whatever the mechanism of packing, it was widely believed that in the construction of the heavier elements some mass remained to be accounted for. Aston's influential book *Isotopes,* published in 1922, merely recorded the commonly held belief that "if hydrogen is transformed into helium a certain quantity of mass must be annihilated in the process. Should the research worker of the future discover some means of releasing the energy in a form which could be employed, the human race will have at its command powers beyond the dreams of science fiction."[29]

The construction of the elements from hydrogen nuclei and electrons was seen not only as possible in principle but as a process actually occurring in the heavens and possibly capable of realization on earth. Ernest Rutherford, invited by Hale to appear before the National Academy of Science in 1915, splendidly summed up the views of many physicists and astrophysicists:

It has been long thought probable that the elements are all built up of some fundamental substances, and Prout's well-known hypothesis that all atoms are composed of hydrogen is one of the best-known examples of this idea.... In the hottest stars the spectra of hydrogen and helium predominate, but with decreasing temperature the spectra become more complicated and the lines of the heavier elements appear.... [I]t is supposed that the light elements combine with decreasing temperature to form the heavier elements. There is no doubt that it will prove a difficult task to bring about the transmutation of matter under ordinary terrestrial conditions. The enormous evolution of energy which accompanies the transformation of radioactive matter affords some indication of the great intensity of the forces that will be required to build up lighter into heavier atoms.[30]

Millikan had long been deeply interested in radioactivity and the problem of the evolution of the elements. His first research program in the new physics concerned these subjects. In a review of the field for *Popular Science Monthly* in 1904, he plainly revealed his enthusiasm: "The dreams of the ancient alchemists are true, for the radio-active elements all appear to be slowly but spontaneously transmuting themselves into other elements." Millikan's noteworthy conclusion lays down a theme to which he would return many times in the succeeding two decades:

The studies of the last eight years upon radiation seem to indicate that in the atomic world also, at least *some* of the heaviest and most complex atomic structures are tending to disintegrate into simpler atoms. The analogy suggests the profoundly interesting question, as to whether or not there is any natural process which does, among the atoms, what the life process does among the molecules, i.e., which takes the simpler forms and builds them up into more complex ones.[31]

The "profoundly interesting question" of a natural process by which complex nuclei are built from simpler ones was part of Millikan's first foray into artificial transmutation in 1912. Millikan and his student George Winchester believed that they had produced hydrogen ions from aluminum by high-voltage discharges.[32] After Sir William Ramsay, Norman Collie, and H. Patterson announced that they thought they had produced helium and neon by means of electrical discharges,[33] Winchester, though not Millikan, suggested in print that while helium and neon were merely occluded gases, *hydrogen* could be liberated from aluminum "in somewhat the same manner as the α particle is disintegrated from radium."[34]

The revolutionary work of Rutherford and James Chadwick in 1919–21 on artificial nuclear transformations created fascinating new possibilities.[35] Deeper understanding of the atom-building process awaited further penetration into the mysteries of the nucleus. Studies of artificial transmutations, it now seemed, offered clues to these mysteries. Millikan followed Rutherford's work with his usual keen and close interest.[36] The possibilities he foresaw were hinted at in an address given in Washington, D.C., shortly before his decision to move permanently to Caltech. His exuberance about the new world of physics just about to be opened was scarcely veiled:

> We have been forced to admit for the first time in history not only
> the possibility but the fact of the growth and decay of the
> elements of matter. With radium and with uranium we do not see
> anything but the decay. And yet somewhere, somehow, it is almost
> certain that these elements must be continually forming. They are
> probably being put together now in the laboratories of the
> stars.... Can we ever learn to control the process? Why not? Only
> research can tell. What is it worth to try it? A million dollars? A
> hundred million? A billion? It would be worth that much if it
> failed, for you could count on more than that amount in by-
> products. And if it succeeded, a new world for man![37]

This "new world for man" and the attempt to come to grips with it contributed to his interest in the construction of the High Voltage Laboratory, and it was this "new world" that Hale had in mind when he wrote of Millikan's interest in this possibility which no other laboratory could match," that is, a laboratory that would enable Millikan "to bust up some of his atoms."[38]

That Millikan intended to use the high-voltage capacities of the proposed laboratory to probe the nucleus as well as for other problems is borne out by the prominence afforded these intentions in the major grant proposals that he and Hale constructed for the Carnegie Corporation of New York in mid-1921. In a preliminary proposal submitted to the corporation's president, James Angell, on June 4, 1921, Hale referred to the High Voltage Laboratory more explicitly as "especially adapted for Dr. Millikan's researches on the breaking-down of atoms and the resolution of the chemical elements into simpler components."[39]

In the fuller grant proposal submitted to the corporation, he revealed that nuclear transformations were to occupy a major place among the concerns of the California Institute of Technology, now emerging as an ambitious center for physical-science research. The heart of the proposal was a joint attack on problems of radiation and matter by the Gates Laboratory and by Hale's Mount Wilson Observatory as well as by Millikan's soon-to-be opened Norman Bridge Laboratory.[40] In their brief summary, Hale, Noyes, and Millikan pointed to several exciting new areas for exploration: radioactive transmutations and the existence of a basic element (hydrogen), direct attention to the possibility of artificial transmutation in the laboratory, and the probability "that in the stars the heavier elements are being built up from the lighter ones, a process not yet realized on earth." The projected physics program included high-potential work bearing on "the nature of atoms and their possible transformations into one another."[41] It is clear that the problem of transmutations was to be approached by a projected research program that was to encompass both heavens and earth, that is, a laboratory attack involving Millikan's plan to "bust up" atoms, and also investigations of stellar processes by the staff of the Mount Wilson Observatory.

A press release, which apparently never saw the light of day, was prepared by Sam Small, Jr., on the basis of interviews with Millikan in 1922: "It is the present task of the scientists at the Institute of Technology, by means of fundamental research working through several directions, to smash the nucleus of the atom and find out what it is made of."[42] Millikan's optimism along these lines continued on into 1923. In an article for *Scribner's Magazine* that year, Millikan reported on the current state of knowledge of the transmutation of elements. "Does the process go on in both directions, heavier atoms being formed as well as continually disintegrating into lighter ones? Not on earth as far as we can see. Perhaps in God's laboratories, the stars." The key question remained: "Can we on earth artificially control the process? To a very slight degree we know already how to *disintegrate* artificially, but not as yet how to build up. As early as 1912, in the Ryerson Laboratory at Chicago, Doctor Winchester and I thought we had good evidence that we were knocking hydrogen out of aluminum and other metals by very powerful electrical discharges in vacuo. We still think our evidence to be good."[43]

Millikan has here made an extraordinary claim. In 1923 he believed that he and Winchester had anticipated Rutherford's artificial transmutation, not as Rutherford had done, with alpha-particle bullets, but with high-voltage discharges.[44] No wonder, then, that Millikan was eager to erect and use a high-voltage laboratory with its million-volt transformer. "How much farther," he continued, "can we go into this artificial transmutation of the elements? This is one of the supremely interesting problems of modern physics *upon which we are all assiduously working.*"[45]

The million-volt transformer was built for the High Voltage Laboratory by Royal Sorensen, professor of electrical engineering at Caltech. Four 250,000-volt, 50-cycle Westinghouse transformers were installed, cascade-fashion, in steel frames, supported by porcelain insulators.[46] But whether the cascade transformer itself was used by Millikan for the study of nuclear transformations is doubtful. It is more likely that he made trials similar to those published by Winchester in 1914. Winchester had built vacuum tubes with an aluminum cathode and platinum anode, and placed high potentials (at that time about 100,000 volts) across them. He generated helium, neon, and hydrogen gases. After careful study he concluded that the neon and helium had been occluded at or near the surface of the electrodes, but that the hydrogen was possibly to be understood as a disintegration product of aluminum. It is reasonable to assume that given his stated interest, Millikan may have made further attempts along these lines in 1922 and 1923, but concluded that the hydrogen, previously identified spectroscopically, was not in fact a disintegration product.[47]

Millikan's plans to smash the nucleus with his high voltage were therefore never successfully prosecuted. In retrospect, with all the advantages of hindsight, even the discussion may seem bizarre. But as we have seen, in the context of the very fluid situation of the early 1920s, Millikan was by no means unjustified in risking some time and research capital. Transmutation was a popular enterprise in the 1920s. Successful attempts to turn base metals into gold by means of medium and high voltages were reported by Adolf Miethe, and H. Stammreich, and Hantaro Nagaoka.[48] Lead was reportedly transmuted into mercury by Andreas Smits of Amsterdam.[49] These claims were vehemently opposed by Fritz Haber and by Francis Aston.[50] Millikan was perhaps too wise an experimentalist to move very far out on this limb.

Millikan turned his energies to a more promising subject that had intrigued him for the better part of a decade. Millikan's search for fuller understanding of the atomic nucleus and its transformations helped to concentrate his efforts in the area that came to be known by the name he himself gave it—cosmic rays.

That a fuller understanding of atom building and the study of astrophysical phenomena were widely seen to be closely related is reflected in Ernest Rutherford's presidential address before the Liverpool meeting of the British Association for the Advancement of Science in September 1923. In this address, Rutherford discussed "another method of attack" on the question of the meaning of artificial transmutation. A close look at the atomic masses of hydrogen and helium shows that "in the synthesis of the helium nucleus from hydrogen nuclei a large amount of energy in the form of radiation has been released in the building of the helium nucleus from its components."[51] Arthur Eddington had suggested that this source of energy may account for the heat emitted by sun and stars. Before the same forum in 1920 Eddington had speculated that the evolution of all other elements from hydrogen occurs in the interiors of stars, and, provocatively, if "the sub-atomic energy in the stars is being freely used to maintain their great furnaces, it seems to bring a little nearer to fulfillment our dream of controlling this latent power for the well-being of the human race—or for its suicide."[52]

Rutherford agreed that the evidence of stellar evolution "certainly indicates that the synthesis of helium, and perhaps other elements of higher atomic weight, may take place slowly in the interior of hot stars."[53] The facilities of the Mount Wilson Observatory, along with those of the Norman Bridge

Laboratory in Pasadena, seemed to place Millikan in a strategic position to investigate these exciting problems.

At this point, around 1922, Millikan welded together his two interests. Until 1922 Millikan's upper-atmosphere research program had emphasized *testing* the existence of rays from space; only at that time did he make explicit his view that the penetrating rays might have their origin in the cosmic processes so interesting to the astrophysicists. The earliest writing yet uncovered in which Millikan makes this connection is his report "Fundamental Researches on the Structure of Matter" for the Carnegie Institution of Washington in 1922: "These penetrating radiations *must apparently have their origins in nuclear changes going on in the atoms of the sun and stars,* and their study is therefore a very fitting part of the program for the joint attack on the problem of the structure of matter from both the physical and the astrophysical points of view."[54]

By 1923 he had also begun to see the penetrating radiation as a link between the nuclear transformations of the elements in the heavens and those occurring on earth. In a paper presented before the Carnegie Institution of Washington titled "Atomic Structure and Etherial Radiation" he made this link explicit. In a letter to John C. Merriam of the Carnegie Institution in 1923 Millikan indicated that he had chosen this topic "because it illustrates the beauty, and the consistency too, of our vision, a vision which has been acquired within the past two decades into the structure of matter, and at the same time the abysmal depths of our ignorance when we attempt to go a little farther and relate these different fields of physical investigation sufficiently to a consistent whole."[55] In the address itself Millikan noted that when "radioactivity was first discovered it was conjectured by some that the energy involved in this radioactive change might come from outside somewhere." Focusing specifically on the energy of beta decay, Millikan posed the important question: "Where does the energy come from which enables the negative electron to push itself out against the pull of the nucleus in which it certainly lies...?" In reply he offered a possible "way out": "I have been interested in recent years because of that difficulty in attempting to find out whether there are any penetrating radiations that come in from the outside."[56]

The notion that the energy for radioactivity might come from "outside somewhere" had first been raised by Marie Curie in 1898. She had suggested that "all space is constantly traversed by rays analogous to Röntgen rays but which are much more penetrating and which can be absorbed only by certain elements of heavy atomic weight such as uranium and thorium."[57] The idea was revived with considerable éclat by Jean Perrin in 1919. Perrin pointed to the known existence of highly penetrating radiation, widely viewed as extraterrestrial in origin, and suggested that these *"rayons ultra X"* were responsible for radioactive dissociation.[58] His views created a flurry of experimental activity, especially after Millikan's work on cosmic rays renewed interest in this area.[59]

During the winter of 1921–22, with the assistance of Ira Bowen and head mechanician Julius Pearson, Millikan had constructed self-recording instruments, weighing only 190 grams, for his balloon flights. Bowen and Millikan sent their equipment aloft from Kelly Field, Texas, in flights that attained altitudes of more than 15 kilometers. The results must have been disappointing. They did not, at least, absolutely confirm the existence of penetrating radiation from above.

Millikan and Bowen sent recording instruments aloft in sounding balloons, each with a barometer, thermometer, and electroscope, which along with the accompanying photographic film weighed only seven ounces. Prevailing views had led them to expect to find very high rates of discharge because only about 12 percent of the atmosphere was left to absorb the radiation. They did not, Millikan reported, "find anything like the computed rates of discharge."[60] They were able to show, however, that if the rays came from above, they were far more penetrating than had been supposed.

Further tests were made in 1922 and 1923 by Millikan and R. Otis from atop Mount Whitney and Pike's Peak, but the results were similarly disappointing and inconclusive.[61] In the *Physical Review* for 1924 Otis and Millikan were able to state only that if one assumed Kolhörster's 1923 conclusions—a penetrating radiation of cosmic origin producing two ions per cubic centime-

Millikan sends instruments aloft. Courtesy of the Archives, California
Institute of Technology.

ter per second and having an absorption coefficient of 2.5×10^{-3} per centimeter in water—the measured ionization was far too low. Moreover, a local storm significantly altered their results. Their conclusions mark a stunning reversal: "We conclude therefore that there exists no such penetrating radiation as we have assumed ... [and] that the whole of the penetrating radiation is of local origin. How such quantities of radioactive material get into the upper air is as yet unkown."[62]

This brief note contains a big surprise: the apparent willingness of Millikan in 1924 to revert to a theory of local radioactive elements as the origin of the penetrating radiation. In June 1924 Millikan lectured at University College, London, and discussed at length "the penetrating radiations of the upper air." The report of the talk in *Nature* confirms the brief *Physical Review* note.[63]

Millikan's skepticism concerning the existence of extra-atmospheric penetrating radiation received support from Gerhard Hoffmann, who likewise thought it arose from known radioelements, and from F. A. Lindemann.[64] Millikan's report to the Carnegie Institution in 1924 rather cryptically referred to the Otis and Millikan results as appearing "to require a profound modification of previous views as to the origin of the penetrating radiation.[65]

In the summer of 1925 Millikan, with his student G. Harvey Cameron, set out to settle the question definitively. They traveled to two California lakes, Muir Lake (altitude 12,000 feet) and Lake Arrowhead (altitude 5,000 feet). They found that the intensity of ionization demonstrated that the rays, coming exclusively from above, had 18 times the penetrating power of the hardest known gamma rays. Sinking their instruments in the upper lake to a depth of 6 feet (the water equivalent in absorbing power of the 7,000 feet of air between the surfaces of the two lakes), they showed that the readings of the lower lake were then identical with that of the upper. They concluded that the atmosphere contributed nothing to the intensity of ionization at the surface of the lower lake. The atmosphere acted only as an "absorbing blanket." The rays came, they said, not from the earth or the atmosphere, but from space.[66] Millikan's skepticism evaporated.

Before the National Academy of Sciences at Madison, Wisconsin, on November 9, 1925, Millikan exuberantly reported on his new findings and dubbed the highly penetrating radiation "cosmic rays." He was quick to return to his earlier cosmic hypotheses. Since the most penetrating rays producible on earth are from radioactive transformations, he reasoned that

> it is scarcely possible, then, to avoid the conclusion that these still more penetrating rays which we have been studying are produced similarly by nuclear transformations of some sort. . . . We can scarcely avoid the conclusion, then, that nuclear changes having an energy value perhaps fifty times as great as the energy changes involved in observed radioactive processes are taking place all through space, and that signals of these changes are being sent to us in these high-frequency rays.[67]

Millikan pointed out that the frequency of the hardest cosmic rays known at that time corresponded to the energy of the formation of helium out of hydrogen, and corresponded closely also to the capture of an electron by a light nucleus. Such nuclear captures might in fact be the likely explanations for the origin of such rays. He was very excited about this evidence for what he saw as the "birth cries" of infant atoms, born either by fusion or by electron capture.[68] Before the American Philosophical Society he exclaimed that we could, if we wished, "call it the music of the spheres!"[69]

The National Academy address excited public attention as little else had previously done in American science. Millikan became, virtually overnight, what would later be called a media figure. The *New York Times* exulted in an editorial: "Dr. R. A. Millikan has gone out beyond our highest atmosphere in search for the cause of a radiation mysteriously disturbing the electroscopes of the physicists," and through "patient, adventuring observations found wild more powerful and penetrating than any that have been domesticated." The *Times* went on to insist that "Millikan rays" ought "to find a place in our planetary scientific directory all the more because they would be associated with a man of such fine and modest personality."[70]

Time magazine seized the occasion to exercise its most purple prose:

> Dr. Robert Andrews Millikan . . . told the Academy about a new ray
> which had been discovered—a ray which begins in eternity. Born
> beyond space, in some dim interstellar vestibule behind the gates
> of the discoverable universe, out of a womb still swollen with gas,
> perhaps with litters of uncreated stars, the Millikan Ray stabs
> earthward, traversing aerial shambles strewn with the débris of
> mutating solar systems, planes where . . . parallel lines may meet,
> and voids in which time, unhinged, spins like a tiny weathervane in
> an everlasting whirlwind.[71]

Within a year and a half, Millikan, inexplicably peering through
a microscope, graced the cover of *Time,* which breathlessly
exclaimed that he had "detected the pulse of the universe."[72]

When Victor Hess expressed chagrin at the use of the term
"Millikan rays" and dismay at the popular success that Millikan
was enjoying as the "discoverer" of penetrating or cosmic
rays,[73] Millikan wrote to him to express regret that the term
was employed, and assured him that "the really important
thing is that between all of us we have been able to make pretty
certain the existence of a radiation which comes to earth from
outside. The evidence for this origin . . . has not been convinc-
ing to a great many physicists including Swann and myself in
this country, Lindemann in England and Hoffmann in Germany.
The evidence seems to me now to be unambiguous. That such
cosmic rays, if they exist, must be of nuclear origin is altogether
obvious. It has been suggested literally scores of times."[74] Millikan's
embarrassment, while genuine, was undoubtedly mixed with
considerable pride and satisfaction in the public acclaim.

In the *Physical Review* for November 1926 Millikan returned
with renewed confidence to the problem of the origin of cosmic
rays. "It is altogether obvious," he wrote, "that any rays of the
hardness and distribution indicated, and of cosmic origin, must
arise from nuclear changes of some sort going on all about the
earth," but far more energetic than any radioactive change thus
far on record. The cosmic rays probably came from among the
following nuclear changes: "(1) the capture of an electron by
the nucleus of a light atom, (2) the formation of helium out of
hydrogen, or (3) some new type of nuclear change, such as the
condensation of radiation into atoms." In any case, the changes
were processes occurring not in stars, but rather, as W. D.

MacMillan of Chicago had suggested, "in the nebulous matter in space, i.e., throughout the depths of the universe."[75] MacMillan had interpreted Millikan's cosmic rays as evidence of "a striking confirmation" of his hypothesis that atoms are being continuously evolved in interstellar space, a view he had discussed with Millikan as early as 1915. "The rays must come," he reaffirmed early in 1928, "in the main from beyond the Milky Way."[76]

By the beginning of March 1928 Millikan was eager to announce another headline-snatching breakthrough. In a letter to his son Glenn dated February 27 he told a remarkable story:

> Night before last about 12:30 I got some new results which gave me quite a fever. Cameron and I had laboriously analyzed our cosmic ray curve and concluded it had to be produced not by general radiation but by bands and we had located three of these bands. These three bands were found Saturday night to fall *just where they should* in the frequency range if they were produced by (1) the formation of helium out of hydrogen, (2) the formation of oxygen out of hydrogen, (3) the formation of silicon out of hydrogen, the three elements which constitute the great bulk of the mass of the earth, of meteorites and of the stars, so far as the latter are amenable to estimates of their constitutions. If these results are valid they constitute the first evidence that the building up as well as the disintegrating process is going on under our eyes, the signal of the birth of an atom of helium, oxygen or silicon being sent out to the ends of the universe wherever such an event occurs in the obstetrical wards of space.... Maybe it is a group of accidental occurrences, but I doubt it!!![77]

Millikan was astonished and excited. His 1904 article for *Popular Science Monthly* titled "Recent Discoveries in Radiation and Their Significance" had posed "a profoundly interesting question": Is there "any natural process which does, among the atoms, what the life process does among the molecules, i.e., which takes the simpler forms and builds them up again into more complex ones?"[78] Now, almost a quarter century later, he hoped—indeed, he more than half believed—that he had the answer at last. Before the California Institute Association in mid-March he elaborated his views.[79] He analyzed the ionization-depth curves that he and Cameron had laboriously compiled. He indicated that the cosmic ray absorption curve could be accounted for by summing the curves of three sets of presumed frequency bands: a low-frequency band, responsible for most of the atmospheric absorption, having an absorption coefficient of 0.35, and two high-frequency bands having coefficients of 0.08 and 0.04. Using the precise work of Aston on atomic weights, Einstein's famous relation between mass and energy, and Paul Dirac's recently published formula for absorption through Compton scattering, he was able to compute energies of the cosmic rays (assumed to be light quanta or photons) of about 25, 110, and 220 million electron volts, and to show that these energies correspond to the "mass defects" that occur in the building up of helium, oxygen, and silicon out of hydrogen.[80] A report in *Science* magazine by Millikan and Cameron declared the cosmic rays photons to be "the announcements sent out through the ether of the birth of the elements."[81]

Writing again to his son Glenn at the end of March, Millikan exulted:

> The philosophy and the science are running together in the new stuff that we have been getting out of cosmic rays....[I]n a nutshell, the thing that looks good is the numerical agreement between observed absorption coefficients and those computed from [the] Einstein equation giving the interrelationship of energy and mass ($mc^2 = E$). The fit seems too good to be a mere coincidence and if it is real it indicates the continuous birth of the ordinary elements out of positive and negative electrons.[82]

Once again the mass media took up Millikan's work as a brilliant illumination of the inner secrets of the universe. The *New York Times'* front page beamed: "Creation Continues, Millikan's Theory"; "Cosmic Rays Herald 'Birth of the Elements'"; even more dramatically, "Super X-Rays Reveal the Secrets of Creation."[83]

When in 1928 the Klein-Nishina formula for relating absorption coefficients with energy replaced Dirac's, Millikan was able to hold fast to his atom-building hypothesis. The revised energy calculations seemed, in fact, to bolster his position.[84] Before the Royal Society, however, Rutherford cautioned that although "the absorption coefficient of the most penetrating radiation

Albert Einstein, Marie Curie, and Millikan, 1924. Courtesy of the Archives, California Institute of Technology.

deduced by Millikan and Cameron from their experiments is in excellent accord with that to be expected on the Klein-Nishina formula for a quantum of energy 940 million volts, we should be wary of relying on extrapolations of theories of absorption into the other energy ranges"; in other words, physicists had little confidence in the formula at energies required for Millikan's interpretations.[85]

The atom-building hypothesis, which Millikan found so exhilarating, at first generated little controversy and even less support among his peers. For Millikan the cosmic photons "must be in fact the birth cries of the elements,"[86] but for others the entire effort seemed contrived. The British physicist E. C. Stoner wrote that the probability of hydrogen atoms' finding each other in order to coalesce was 'vanishingly small.'"[87]

James Chadwick, soon to discover the neutron, roundly criticized Millikan's atom-building hypothesis and its methodology at a Royal Society "Discussion on Ultra-Penetrating Rays," when he noted that the separation of the radiation into components was "a questionable proceeding, for other interpretations of the absorption curve are possible"; furthermore, he thought it unlikely that the Klein-Nishina formula was valid for the penetrating rays.[88] When (as we shall see in Chapter 6) during the course of the 1930s the work of Arthur H. Compton and others demonstrated that cosmic rays were not photons at all, but were in fact composed of charged particles, the underpinnings of the atom-building hypothesis collapsed. Indeed, Millikan and his co-worker Carl Anderson themselves directly measured cosmic ray energies in 1931 and found them to be far in excess of any that could be accounted for by packing fractions, or loss of mass in atom building.[89] He began, at this point, a slow retreat to a fall-back position; from atom building he and his co-workers ultimately passed to atom annihilation.[90]

But for Millikan during the late 1920s, the atom-building hypothesis was a striking confirmation of his faith in an evolving atomic structure, that is, one in which atoms were being constructed as well as radioactively decaying. It was a way to avoid the "heat death" or running down of the universe posed by the second law of thermodynamics,[91] and, even if he retreated from this position, at least it was in his eyes "a little bit of *experimental* finger-pointing" toward a Creator who was continually on the job.[92] In short, atom building was an idea in deep harmony with Millikan's fundamental spiritual yearnings. In 1904 the evolution of the elements, as suggested by radioactivity, was for him a way of rejecting crass materialism; as he later expressed it: "*Matter* is no longer a mere game of marbles played by blind men. An atom is now an amazingly complicated organism, possessing many interrelated parts and exhibiting many functions and properties—energy properties, radiating properties, wave properties, and other properties quite as mysterious as any that used to masquerade under the name of 'mind'. Hence the phrases—'All is matter' and 'All is mind'—have now become more shibboleths completely devoid of meaning."[93] By the early 1920s these beliefs became issues. The resurgence of Protestant fundamentalism in the form of an antiscientific crusade forced the problem to the front of his conscience. William Jennings Bryan, among others, began a forceful campaign against evolution; he was abetted by such flamboyant evangelists as Billy Sunday and Aimee Semple McPherson. An article of Bryan's, "God and Evolution," which appeared in the *New York Times* on February 26, 1922, touched a nerve among scientists and modernist theologians. Among those who evinced alarm was Robert E. Brown, a Congregationalist minister and Millikan's brother-in-law. Brown blamed both the Bryanites and the Darwinians for the current tempest. He deplored the ignorant attacks made on evolution, but denigrated as well much scientific pedagogy that was "too often in the hands of men who are not in sympathy with religious ideals." He called on scientists to declare openly that evolution is not antireligion. "You have been generous enough," he wrote to Millikan, "to say that a declaration from Congregationalist ministers in favor of evolution would have its influence. But I want to tell you that it would be as nothing if men like you ... would make some such declaration."[94]

Brown pursued the point more vigorously a month later:

Now can't you do something to reach a hand across the gap to us? No scientific congress would probably want to express sympathy with sane religion although it would be powerfully effective if you would. Could you not draw up a set of resolutions and have some scientific body go as far as you can get them to go? If not can you not draw up some kind of a document and have it signed by all the scientists you know who are sympathetic with moral and spiritual ideals? Men like yourself, Professor [Edwin G.] Conklin, [Herbert] Osborn, and perhaps Einstein and [Hendrik A.] Lorentz. You could do much to help steady the situation among the Baptists and encourage liberal men to keep up the fight.... Bryan's guns would be spiked![95]

Brown's appeal had special relevance for Millikan, who had been disturbed since his arrival in Pasadena by California fundamentalism. Aimee Semple McPherson had been conducting her revivals for some time, and in 1923 would found her Angelus Temple in Los Angeles for the spread of her Four Square Gospel. The fourth annual convention of the World's Christian Fundamentals Association met in July 1922 in Los Angeles to attack "evolution and modernism" and in 1924 began a series of attacks on biology textbooks in the schools.[96] In 1925 Paul Rood began his Bryan Bible League in California and ultimately became an officer of the World's Christian Fundamentals Association.[97] The Scopes trial in 1925 would also soon add to Millikan's concern.

But in mid-1923 his brother-in-law's reaction to Bryan sufficed. Millikan formulated a draft statement, which was revised by Arthur Noyes[98] and signed by religious leaders, including Brown and Henry Churchill King, president of Oberlin College; by such scientists as Osborn, Conklin, Michael I. Pupin, J. J. Carty, Millikan, Noyes, William Welch, John C. Merriam, Gano Dunn, and William W. Campbell; and by such men of public affairs as Herbert Hoover, secretary of commerce, and James John Davis, secretary of labor.[99] The dominance of the NRC group is clearly evident.

A critical part of the statement was Millikan's, and reflected his concern with "living" matter and the evolution of the elements: "It is a sublime conception of God which is furnished by science, and one wholly consonant with the highest ideals of religion, when it represents Him as revealing Himself through countless ages in the development of the earth as an abode for man and in the age-long inbreathing of life into its constituent matter, culminating in man with his spiritual nature and all his God-like powers."[100] The key passage concerns Millikan's belief in "the age-long in-breathing of life into its constituent matter," a belief that ties together this ongoing interest in radioactivity, his quarter-century search for evidence of atom building, and his faith in man's spiritual nature. In short, the stage was set long before for his "discovery" of the energy bands in cosmic rays and his interpretation of them.

Millikan elaborated on his scientific-religious views in the

Terry Lectures in 1927, given at Yale and published under the title *Evolution in Science and Religion*. Once again the centrality of evolution or progress from lower to higher forms is clearly evident: "Through the careful study of the way the rocks lie on our hillsides we have found evidence for the growth of this earth through a billion years at the least. Through the study of radioactivity and other physical processes we have found definite evidence that the world is evolving and changing all the time, even in its chemical elements ... a *new conception of progress has entered the thought of the world,* a progress in which we play an important part."

For Millikan, it was not only the teachings of science as the key to God's universe that were of critical importance. Along with his natural theology, the *practice* of science, too, resonated with his Christianity: "The practical preaching of modern science—and it is the most insistent and effective preacher in the world today—is extraordinarily like the preaching of Jesus. Its keynote is service, the subordination of the individual to the good of the whole. Jesus preached it as a duty—for the sake of world-salvation. Science preaches it as a duty—for the sake of world-progress."

The verse—and the long hours—that Millikan brought to his research were likewise expressible in the language of Christian religion: "Jesus also preached the joy and the satisfaction of service. 'He that findeth his life shall lose it, and he that loseth his life ... shall find it.' When the modern scientist says he does it 'for the fun of it' or 'for the satisfaction he gets out of it,' he is only translating the words of Jesus into the modern vernacular."[101]

In "What I Believe" for *Forum* magazine, he summed up his credo: "There are three ideas which seem to stand out above all others in the influence they have exerted upon the development of the human race.... They are the following—1. The idea of the Golden Rule; 2. The idea of natural law; 3. The idea of age-long growth or evolution."[102] Millikan's "God of Science is the Spirit of rational order, and of orderly development";[103] responding to a query from a *Time* reporter, he said, "Science dominated by the spirit of religion is the key to progress and the hope of mankind."[104]

A noted historian of American science has called Millikan "a Babbitt who became a Nobel laureate in physics."[105] To be sure, Millikan was a conservative, a Hoover Republican, a man who enjoyed the ease with which he moved among the powerful and wealthy, but he was not a hollow man. The essence of Babbittry is its empty and small-minded materialism; Millikan was moved by a larger spirit and deeper values. His vision was shaped in the nineteenth century and bears its mark. He believed in an America redeemed by the hard work of God-fearing folk; he worked for an America in which science and religion moved together to define progress. Those of us who do not share his vision are forced, at least, to acknowledge its existence.

The decade of the 1920s marked the apogee of Millikan's public career. At age sixty in 1928, he was chief executive of one of America's most vital institutions of higher education and research, he was still active in research programs at or near the frontiers of his discipline, and he had become a recognized spokesman for science in the United States.[106] He looked and acted the part: *Time* magazine described him as a "man of twinkling blue-gray eyes and sparkling wit [who] knows how to make scientific complexities charming as well as awesome."[107] He began to speak out on a wide variety of public issues. He addressed the nation not only on religion, but also increasingly in the decade after 1925 on science and industry, modern life, Edison, humanism, unemployment, peace, the future, "excess" government, education, civilization, the standard of living, and social justice.[108] He was a much sought-after lecturer on radio and in public forums. John Finley of the *New York Times* rather extravagantly wrote to him, "There is no voice in the cosmos that is more persuasive than yours."[109] He was, with the exception of Albert Einstein, the most famous scientist of his day in America. He was—a celebrity.

The willingness of Americans to *listen* attests to much more than Millikan's personal success. The popular prestige of science during the 1920s had risen rapidly. The "informal" history by Frederick Lewis Allen, *Only Yesterday*, relates the temper of the time: "The prestige of science was colossal. The man in the street and the woman in the kitchen, confronted on every hand with new machines and devices which they owed to the labora-

The sage. Courtesy of the Archives, California Institute of Technology.

tory, were ready to believe that science could accomplish almost anything." The Scientist became the bearer of civilization and purveyor of progress. "The word science had become a shibboleth. To preface a statement with 'Science teaches us' was enough to silence argument. If a sales manager wanted to put over a promotion scheme or a clergyman to recommend a charity, they both hastened to say that it was scientific."[110] The scientist had become a sage.

The popular ideology of science so colorfully described by Allen was deeply rooted in real transformations in American life. The effects of the scientific-technical revolution were being felt ever more strongly in the years between the wars. Scientific agriculture and science-based industry had made impressive advancements; scientific medicine was making bold promises; the first shock of scientific warfare was barely over. It is no exaggeration to claim that the permeation of science into the hidden places of public and private life was a process already far along.

Between 1907 and 1925 the real income of the average American had risen dramatically. Science and technology were generally given credit for that, as well as for the internal combustion engine, electrification, radio, the airplane, medical X rays, pharmaceuticals, chemical fertilizers, and so forth. Babbitt's "god was Modern Appliances," conveniences that most people agreed were the fruits of science.[111]

Science had defined modernity. Walter Lippmann expressed the matter succinctly and eloquently: "Because the scientific discipline is, in fact, the creative element in that which is distinctively modern, circumstances conspire to enhance its prestige and to extend its acceptance. It is the ultimate source of profit and power.... The scientific discipline has become... an essential part of our social heritage. For the machine technology requires a population which in some measure partakes of the spirit which created it."[112] For many Americans, Robert Andrews Millikan epitomized that spirit.

6

Recessional

Man with his burning soul
Has but an hour of breath
To build a ship of Truth
In which his soul may sail,
Sail on the sea of death.
For death takes toll
Of beauty, courage, youth,
Of all but Truth.
                    —John Masefield

This quotation from Masefield's "Truth" was a favorite of Millikan's. Indeed, he came to see his scientific work as monuments to Truth, as enduring contributions to a great, permanent enterprise. One may understand his defensiveness when younger critics began to appear on the physics scene during the late 1920s and early 1930s. He doubtless overreacted in 1926 to Edward U. Condon's little piece on cosmic rays in the *Proceedings* of the National Academy of Sciences, which, Millikan thought, implied criticism of his use of the absorption coefficient. Millikan's very testy letter to the young man claimed that the paper assumed "complete stupidity on the part of the observer."[1] When Raymond Birge's early reevaluations of the electron charge were presented to him in 1929, he retorted "that if you are going to do this...you have only made a beginning and will have to do it a good deal more thoroughly and less superficially.... Your review will be improved by a less contentious tone and a less dogmatic assertiveness of wrongness and rightness."[2] He seemed to believe that attempts to refine his measurements were indirect attacks on his character or intelligence. Such a defensive attitude was ill served by William Brittain's *Scienservice* report on the work of Erik Bäcklin, whose X-ray crystal measurements implied a value for e that differed from Millikan's. The report virtually screamed "scandal":

MIGHTY ELECTRON GIVES SCIENCE NEW SENSATION
Latest Work Proves Millikan was Awarded
Nobel Prize for a Mistake, Physicists Say[3]

Millikan was justifiably outraged and called the article "the worst type of yellow journalism" and "the prostitution of science to sensationalism."[4] Brittain wrote to apologize. But the report was only the opening shot in a decade-long campaign against the results of the oil-drop experiment.

X-ray wavelength measurements by means of crystal lattices were by the late 1920s, very precise; precision measurements by an alternative method—the ruled grating method—ought to have been just as precise. Bäcklin found, however, that for a given X ray the two methods produced different results. The crystal method employed a constant (Avogadro's number, the number of molecules in a mole of a substance) that had been derived from Millikan's value for the electron charge. Bäcklin suggested that the discrepancy was accounted for not by a fault in either method, but rather by a fault in the *constant,* and therefore in Millikan's value for the charge of the electron. He came up with a value for e that was about one-half of 1 percent higher than Millikan's determination.[5]

Also employing the X-ray method was J. Alvin Bearden, a former student of Compton at Chicago, and by then a faculty member at Johns Hopkins. Bearden undertook a series of experiments, the earliest public statement of which came at a meeting of the Physical Society in Washington, D.C., in April 1929. Millikan attended, and upon hearing the results became incensed. Bearden reports that Millikan was very hostile to the young "upstart" who was attempting to undermine his achievement. After the Brittain *Scienservice* episode, Millikan's sensibilities were doubtless especially tender. Bearden informed President J. S. Ames of Johns Hopkins that he intended to ask Millikan to discuss the matter personally; Ames warned him that Millikan would kill his career.[6] But Bearden persisted and had a lengthy and actually friendly interview with Millikan at the National Academy building in Washington. Millikan remained, however, unconvinced concerning the new value of *e*.

His prestige seemed for a while to carry the day. Raymond Birge's careful assessments of physical constants in 1929 and 1932 concluded that Millikan's value for *e* was still the one most acceptable.[7] But the battle was far from over. Kamekichi Shiba published in 1932 a forceful critique of the problem of constants. Shiba was totally convinced that the discrepancies between the crystal and ruled grating methods stemmed from Millikan's value of *e*, and suggested that the source of the inaccuracy was Millikan's determination of the constant η, the viscosity of air.[8] Millikan had done his own measurements for this constant, but it was generally agreed that his student Ertle Harrington had done the most precise measurement.[9] Shiba pointed out that if a higher value for the viscosity was employed, the Millikan value could be brought into line with the required X-ray value for *e*. Much later, in 1937, W. V. Houston showed that Harrington had overlooked certain viscous drag corrections that had to be made to reach a proper determination of the viscosity of air—corrections that when made raised the value of η, and raise Millikan's value by about 0.6 percent.[10] In 1935 Bearden's further work had given a new figure for *e*—$(4.8036 \pm 0.0005)10^{-10}$ e.s.u.—which was generally accepted.[11] At the time, Millikan made little comment, but in his *Autobiography*— rather reluctantly, it seems—he makes note of the importance of Bearden's work.[12]

Even his Caltech colleagues were not exempt from Millikan's suspicions. J. Robert Oppenheimer, for whose ability Millikan was known to have great respect, believed himself to be maltreated after he and J. T. Carlson presented a paper at the New Orleans meeting of the Physical Society in December 1931. In the paper Oppenheimer and Carlson raised doubts about the photon character of cosmic rays, and suggested the possibility that they might be composed of Wolfgang Pauli's suggested "neutron."[13] No direct evidence of Millikan's reaction has yet been uncovered, but shortly thereafter Oppenheimer wrote to Ernest O. Lawrence at Berkeley that he was "distressed by Millikan's hostility and his lack of scruple."[14]

Chafing as the electron charge debates were, an even more discomfiting public challenge came from another quarter. In 1930 Arthur H. Compton, winner of the Nobel Prize in physics for 1927, began a massive effort in the area of cosmic rays. By the end of 1931 he had secured for it significant funding from the Carnegie Institution of Washington. His aim was primarily to study variations in the intensity of cosmic rays around the entire globe, with special emphasis on discerning a "latitude effect," that is, the effect of the earth's magnetic field on the intensities of cosmic rays. The general goal was to "learn more definitely regarding the nature and origin of the rays."[15] In 1927 Jakob Clay had found variations in the intensities of cosmic rays in Java and the Netherlands; he ascribed the differences to the differential effects of the earth's magnetism at the two latitudes.[16] If the cosmic rays were photons or light rays, as Millikan and most others believed, the earth's magnetic field ought to have no effect on them, for they are *uncharged*. If it could be shown that the magnetic field was indeed affecting the intensities, it would be strong evidence that the primary rays were *charged* particles, like protons, electrons, or helium nuclei. The so-called latitude effect was, then, an important test case. Other observers failed at first to confirm Clay,[17] but Carl Störmer and, later, G. Lemaitre and M. L. Vallarta demonstrated how in fact the earth's magnetic field could account quantitatively for the variations in the rays' intensity.[18] Compton had considerable reason, therefore, for his hunch that Millikan was wrong, and for his decision to ask for considerable resources to mount a campaign against prevailing opinion and attempt to verify the latitude effect.[19]

By the first of February 1932 Compton had assembled nine groups under various leaders, including Admiral Richard E. Byrd, who was assigned the task of recording measurements in the Antarctic. Compton himself traveled to Hawaii, Canada, and Latin America; others were responsible for the Punjab and Mount McKinley, in Alaska. Despite two tragic accidents, which took the lives of three expedition members, the results came quickly and dramatically. In September 1932 the *New York Times* ran the arresting headline: "HOLDS MILLIKAN IS WRONG." Compton was quoted as saying, "My work on the arctic barren lands show the cosmic ray is an electron, not a wave as Dr. Millikan believes.... The difference shown by my experiments will be a severe blow to Dr. Millikan."[20] If Compton was quoted correctly, he took an unnecessarily aggressive attitude toward Millikan, and introduced an ad hominem character to the debate that Millikan was to find deplorable. It was true, however, that if Compton's results were substantiated, they *would* constitute a severe blow to Millikan and a shattering attack on the atom-building hypothesis he held so dear. The atom-building hypothesis depended fundamentally on Millikan's basic view that the primary cosmic rays were electromagnetic energy (photons or light waves) arising from the conversion of mass to energy in the fusion process rather than charged particles. The *Times* highlighted the cosmic implications: Compton's findings would be a test case for viewing the universe as constantly renewing itself through the building up of atoms or moving toward the "heat death" of which the popular press so liked to remind its readers.

Compton was very confident. In the Carnegie Institution's yearbook for 1931–32 he emphatically stated that "the cosmic rays do depend upon the earth's magnetic field.... This discovery presents strong evidence in favor of the view that the cosmic rays are streams of electrified particles such as electrons or protons."[21] Millikan responded in characteristic fashion. He mounted his own expedition to the Arctic and he sent a Caltech Ph.D., H. Victor Neher, on a survey from Los Angeles to Mollendo, Peru, to attempt to demonstrate the nonexistence of the latitude effect. Millikan indeed found no latitude effect, and Neher cabled Millikan twice, from Balboa on November 10 and from Mollendo on November 20, both times with the same message: "No change."[22] Millikan's enthusiasm was restored. Before the Astronomical and Physical Club at Caltech on December 2, 1932, he emphatically denied the existence of the latitude effect and expressed renewed confidence in his own views on the nature and origin of cosmic rays.[23] To Compton he was more subdued. He believed that Neher's results would help to avoid confrontation at the forthcoming symposium on cosmic rays at Atlantic City. He wrote to Compton: "There is nothing left for controversy at Atlantic City and we can keep the Atlantic City discussion off from the controversial field."[24]

The Carnegie Institution of Washington, under President John Campbell Merriam, a longtime Hale-Millikan-Noyes ally, likewise moved to manage the potential conflict. In December 1932 Merriam appointed a Committee on the Coordination of Cosmic Ray Investigations to monitor and mediate between the two Carnegie star investigators, Millikan and Compton. Walter S. Adams, of Mount Wilson, Sir John Ambrose Fleming, and Frederick E. Wright were asked to serve. The committee's report noted that "while it is recognized that a certain amount of scientific competition is desirable and must be encouraged, the deliberations certainly brought out clearly the need of definite collaboration and cooperation to clarify not only the problems but also the interpretation of results."[25] A conflict, however, was not to be avoided. Thomas Johnson, a noted young cosmic physicist, knew that the cosmic ray symposium of the American Association for the Advancement of Science in Atlantic City would be "hot...for Millikan has a chip on his shoulder and Compton is...[ready] to knock it off."[26]

The *New York Times* account of the meeting seems to indicate that Johnson's expectations were correct: "MILLIKAN RETORTS HOT-LY TO COMPTON IN COSMIC RAY CLASH." The story went on: "Dr. Millikan particularly sprinkled his talk with remarks directly aimed at his antagonist's scientific acumen. There was an obvious coolness between the two men when they met after the debate was over."[27] Millikan denied this report in strong terms,[28] but when William Laurence, a *Times* reporter, tried to get the two to shake hands, Millikan refused.

Fate had conspired with his own supreme confidence to play a trick. In the region of Los Angeles, as it later became clear, the dip in cosmic ray intensity began suddenly off the coast and reached its maximum within two days' sail. Unfortunately, Neher had trouble setting up his electroscope, and did not get it to work until he had already passed the region of the dip. On the return voyage, however, Neher did indeed measure the latitude effect, and so informed Millikan at Atlantic City, but it was already too late.[29]

The *Nation* acidly commented that "Drs. Millikan and Compton, the two Nobel Prize winners, clashed acrimoniously.... It is obvious enough that there was more heat than light in the argument which revolved around stupendous deductions from highly dubious data. The true explanation is, of course, that Drs. Millikan and Compton are really discussing religion while they pretend to discuss science."[30]

Millikan was forced to retreat on the question of the existence of the latitude effect. His interpretation of it, however, was now tailored to fit his well-known views. At first he would insist that the *primary* cosmic rays were photons; the charged particles implied by the latitude effect were *secondaries,* or particles produced by the action of the first. Before the London Conference on Nuclear Physics in 1934, of which he was copresident, Millikan held to his photon interpretation of cosmic rays: "We may conclude with certainty that... all but a very small part of the ionization of the air is due to secondaries produced within the atmosphere."[31] His audience was unimpressed. Now that new evidence demonstrated the existence of cosmic rays far more energetic than could be accounted for by the atom-building theory, Millikan began to modify his stance on the origins of the rays—but ever so slightly. He insisted before the conference that the only cause of such energetic photons could be the annihilation of matter according to Einstein's law ($E = mc^2$) *either* within the compass of the atom-building process *or* (as had been suggested before by others) by the total annihilation of atoms.[32]

In an interview with Donald Caley in October 1934, Millikan expanded on his turn toward annihilation as a possible theory of the origins of cosmic rays. "We now know," he said, "that there are some very penetrating components of the rays which have energies higher than those that can correspond to any such transformation of mass into radiant energy as occurs when the heaviest elements that we know anything about are assumed to be suddenly formed out of the process of suddenly building them up out of hydrogen." Resurrecting the atom-annihilation view, he commented: "That such a complete annihilation of the whole of the atom can take place all at once will be doubted by many physicists and astronomers and I am far from asserting that it does. But it nevertheless is true that there is no other tenable source of energy in sight that will yield the cosmic ray energies which we actually observe."[33]

By 1935 Millikan could no longer totally resist the strong evidence about the nature of the rays. In an article for *Science*, "What to Believe about Cosmic Rays," he admitted that cosmic rays "have some of these charged particles as constituents." He went on to claim: "There has never been any doubt about that in anybody's mind so far as I know."[34] Now, for Millikan, the cosmic rays were a mixture of photons and charged particles; his opponents deemed the photons to constitute less than 1 percent of the total.

During 1935 Millikan produced a greatly expanded revision of his book *The Electron*, newly titled *Electrons (+ and –), Protons, Photons, Neutrons, Mesotrons, and Cosmic Rays*. His cosmic ray chapters are notoriously self-justifying. By careful selection his own role and the parts played by his colleagues and collaborators were greatly enhanced, and those of his opponents reduced markedly. In the subsection on the latitude effect, for instance, Arthur Compton's name does not appear. Jakob Clay's important contribution is accorded only second place, following some results that Dr. Oliver Gish "reported to me" in 1928. "Also Clay in 1927 and 1928...had reported at least a 15% drop."[35] On the critical question of the origin of cosmic rays, Millikan held fast to his view that cosmic rays were produced as photons, but produce secondary electrons in space. The penetrating radiation impinging on earth, therefore, contains both photons and electrons:

> Whenever in their travel through space they have gone through matter, even though in the creative act they were sent forth as pure photons, they have necessarily produced secondary electron rays such as we find them producing in our terrestrial electroscopes, so that there is no existing theory of the origin of the cosmic ray that does not require, once the existence of the cosmic ray photons is postulated at all, that space be traversed both by these photons and by the secondary electrons.... In other words, the rays which enter the earth must in any case be a mixture of photons and extra-terrestrial secondary electrons.[36]

On these issues Millikan was isolated, except for his loyal Caltech band. He defended himself by denying the existence of error, implying priority, and stressing the continuity of his past views with recent research. That "ship of Truth" of the Masefield poem of which he was so fond, that ship "on which his soul may sail," was in danger of foundering. It was a trying time. A former Caltech student, now a noted scientist, recalls Millikan as inordinately fond of showing his medals, and especially proud of one bestowed by the pope.[37] He was wrapping himself in past glory.

The appearance of his book *Electrons (+ and −)* early in 1935 touched some sensitive nerves in the profession. Millikan's stubborn refusal to agree with what was emerging as a consensus on cosmic ray issues, and his single-minded concentration on his own contributions and those of his collaborators, elicited criticism from many quarters. L. G. H. Huxley's review of the book in *Nature* said:

> Perhaps the least satisfactory section of the book is the chapter on the nature of cosmic rays. . . . The treatment of the subject matter seems to be directed towards establishing the hypothesis that the primary radiation is composed principally of photons, a view of its nature not generally accepted. Consequently other investigators are treated quite summarily. For example Clay's discovery of the latitude effect and Compton's organised world survey which confirmed it receive but scanty attention.[38]

The review of the book by Edward U. Condon in the *Review of Scientific Instruments,* while generally more restrained, provided some pungent comment: "Some will criticize the account as emphasizing too strongly Millikan's own work and that of his associates. The thought suggests itself that the book should have as subtitle, 'Happy Days and Nights in the Norman Bridge Laboratory.'"[39]

The widely noticed slights to other workers formed the background to acrimonious exchange between Millikan, on the one hand, and Arthur Compton and Jakob Clay, on the other. The occasion for the controversy was the publication in 1935 and 1936 of two articles by Millikan and his co-worker Victor

Neher concerning "geographic" effects on cosmic ray intensity. The first stated that Millikan and Neher had announced the evidence for the "hitherto unsuspected" longitude effect in April 1934, relegating to a footnote this information: "Professor Clay informs us by letter that he made the discovery of the longitude effect independently."[40] Clay reported his results briefly in *Physica* in March 1934, and more fully in the same journal in August of that year.

The second article concerned a new worldwide survey to investigate the latitude effect. Again Millikan makes no mention of Compton's famous and influential survey.[41] Both articles continue the tone of the previous articles and the book. Neither gives the reader a satisfactory picture of the state of science. Both Compton and Clay therefore had grounds for annoyance when they began to collaborate on a two-part article that would expose what to them were Millikan's transgressions.

The opening shot was a letter from Compton to Millikan enclosing a copy of the joint Compton-Clay effort. The letter was stiff and formal, informing Millikan that they wished to publish the two-part article "in order to clarify the position of the other students of the geographic distribution of cosmic rays." The handwritten postscript was rather more conciliatory, congratulating Millikan on Carl Anderson's Nobel prize, and adding, "It might just as properly have been a joint award to Anderson and yourself."[42] Compton's paper, however, roundly criticized Millikan and Neher for "their inadequate consideration of the work of others"; Clay's paper noted: "I fail to understand why Millikan in recent years has not followed the common practice in science of comparing his own results with those of other works in the same field."[43]

Millikan's reply was understandably irritable. Compton's article, he wrote, "is so replete with misstatements...and so ad hominum [sic] from beginning to end—that I think it will have a disastrous influence if published upon the esteem in which science and scientists are held by the public."[44]

After an unsuccessful effort to find an impartial mediator acceptable to both sides, and with the advice of A. J. Dempster, Compton toned down his paper. He hoped to avoid what Millikan had called ad hominem remarks. While in the original draft Compton referred to Millikan and Neher's paper on the latitude effect as an "extensive series of measurements," in the second draft he inserted after "extensive" the words "and valuable." Whereas in the first version he wrote of the "fact that the authors have failed to refer to any except one of the many earlier studies of the same subject by other investigators," the second draft merely notes that "the authors have refrained from referring to the many articles of a similar type that have recently been published."[45]

Millikan was not yet mollified. In a letter dated January 19, 1937, he wrote: "You think I have shown my incapacity to deal properly with your work; and I am certain that during the last five years you have demonstrated your incapacity either to understand my work or to handle it in a way which seems to me to possess the first element of correct scientific treatment." He added, "Much more might and indeed should be written if this stupid and demeaning controversy must be continued."[46]

Ultimately Compton had neither the endurance nor the appetite for what he began to see as a counterproductive squabble. He withdrew his paper and wrote to Millikan: "When I realized that the publication of my article might really hinder the effectiveness of your work, I could not but agree that its appearance was inadvisable."[47] Compton's letter ended the fracas. He knew that Millikan was already far along a blind alley, and there was no need to badger him from behind. The center of cosmic ray research was no longer at Millikan's hand. But Clay, without the advantages of Compton's prestige or perspective, remained bitter: "I am forced to have the worst idea of the character of Mr. Millikan as I have seen he is violating the truth, as he does, for his own profit without any scruples."[48]

It is curious but not surprising that Millikan at one point termed Compton's attack a "use of the 'smear Hoover' type of technique."[49] It is a small bit of evidence concerning Millikan's feelings of political as well as scientific isolation. During the Harding and Coolidge administrations Millikan appeared supremely comfortable. He was an enthusiastic supporter of Herbert Hoover's presidential ambitions in 1928; no one was more delighted than he by the success of Hoover's candidacy. In 1932 he was willing to enter the lists and actively campaign for his friend and former colleague on the National Research Council and National Research Endowment. In Millikan's eyes, Hoover was a leader who applied "the scientific method of approach to governmental problems."[50]

For Millikan, the scientific method, applied to the problems of economic and civic life, was the key to orderly change and improvement. Opposed to the New Deal and increasingly estranged from the federal government under Roosevelt, Millikan opted instead for those patterns of influence in which he participated in the 1920s and which he believed still to be successful. "The only real *progressive* is the man who is using the scientific method—the only method which has led to progress in the past, and who casts his influence always in favor of those who are carefully and scientifically trained."[51] The Depression? The economic woe of America was "temporarily a jam in the social machinery which makes it impossible at the moment to reap the benefit of the scientist and the engineer in creating more wealth."[52] He refused to see the blacker side of the hard times. "Call unemployment leisure and one can at once see the possibilities."[53] In fact, he asserted often, "The common man . . . is vastly better off here today in depressed America than he has ever been at any other epoch in society."[54]

In the vein of Hoover's *American Individualism* (1920), Millikan preferred the route of "community self-help," the pioneer mix of self-reliance and local solidarity that had won the frontier.[55] Indeed, there was a clear danger from the New Deal. Too much paternalism would rot the fiber of the nation. "Some call this communism, some socialism, some something else, but I will use the word 'statism' to include the whole tendency for the government's ownership and operation of everything." This statism, he continued, "weakens self-reliance, discourages private initiative, diminishes opportunity."[56]

In a radio address for the National Broadcasting Company in 1934, "Excess Government May Spoil the American Dream," he invoked that "great thinker" Herbert Spencer, who "called socialism the coming slavery."[57] Big government was an encroaching evil, and so was big labor. Millikan was against pro-union New Deal legislation: "Economic forces [are] enormously more potent than man-made laws."[58] But the immediate task was to oppose the "political royalists," who were more sinister than the economic royalists: "The usurpation by the central government in the United States of the power of the states and the local communities [is] ominous."[59]

In the 1940 election campaign, as expected, Millikan spoke against Franklin Roosevelt, who he believed was "Tammanyizing the United States."[60] The American patronage system, so corrupt and so damaging, must be destroyed. It was a theme to which he would return again and again: government corruption through the patronage system was fatally weakening America. In such talks as "The Preservation of Freedom" he would inveigh against the evils of "the corrupt patronage system."[61]

It is no surprise, then, that Millikan vehemently opposed the efforts of scientists and politicans to establish a national system of support for science in the wake of World War II. As early as 1942, Senator Harley Kilgore of West Virginia had introduced a Technology Mobilization Bill that aimed at establishing an Office of Technological Mobilization to aid the war effort. By 1943 Kilgore's goals had broadened; he reintroduced a Science Mobilization Bill, strenuously opposed by the science leadership, including Millikan's friend Frank Jewett, president of the National Academy of Sciences and former head of Bell Laboratories, who said that scientists were opposed "to being made the intellectual slaves of the State."[62] After the conclusion of the war, Kilgore's bill evolved into an act to establish the National Science Foundation, to fund and coordinate research and development in America, with an emphasis on work useful to the nation. The foundation was to be headed by a director chosen by the president. The results of government-sponsored research would belong to the nation. The Kilgore bill would support the social as well as the natural sciences. It was supported by many influential scientists, including Harold Urey, Edward U. Condon, and Harlow Shapley.

Many elements of the Kilgore bill, however, disturbed much of the scientific leadership. Vannevar Bush, director of the wartime Office of Scientific Research and Development (OSRD), moved to erect a rival program. Like the Kilgore program, Bush's program accepted the principle of national funding and coordination of research and development. Bush opposed, however, the enormous control by the president over scientific planning which the Kilbore bill would have instituted. He opposed its patent policy and its inclusion of the social sciences on a par with the natural sciences. Bush's own program was sponsored by Senator Warren Magnuson of Washington. At the hearings for both the Kilgore and Magnuson bills, ninety-eight of ninety-nine witnesses endorsed the principle of government support for science and a national effort along the lines outlined in both bills. The lone exception was again Frank Jewett, Millikan's confidant and NRC crony, who preferred the more traditional, private funding schemes for science:

> It seems to me that if you set up a Federal corporation and furnish it with funds to spend in a particular sector of our economy, you are not only running the danger of overstimulating but you are certainly inviting the formation of pressure groups in the other sectors—the social sciences or a thousand and one other things—who feel they have a valid claim of special treatment, and you are going to be confronted, in my judgment, in the not very distant future, with urgent claims to set up corresponding corporations to fructify other fields.[63]

In February 1946 Kilgore introduced a compromise bill (S. 1850) which retained the emphasis on national utility and presidential direction, but, by giving way on smaller items, appeared to have a reasonable chance of passage. In the House, Representative Wilbur Mills proposed a bill more along the lines of the Bush program, and Senator Raymond Willis of Indiana introduced a new bill drafted in the main by Jewett. It was obviously a stripped-down, bare-bones measure aimed strictly at blocking Kilgore. This bill (S. 1777) proposed the establishment of a self-perpetuating committee of fifty, chosen by the president from a list submitted by the National Academy of Sciences, that would administer a program of limited scientific activity.[64] Millikan watched the progress of the bills closely. He wrote Jewett, "I was greatly pleased that your activity had been responsible for the stirring up of some kind of science bill which is not so loaded with political implications as both the Magnuson or Kilgore bills." Of course, *no* bill would be preferable to any bill. Federal involvement risked "leading us further into totalitarianism."[65]

Even at seventy-eight, Millikan was active in lining up support for the Willis bill; he reported to Jewett, "I got approval from...[Max] Mason, Munro [W. S.] Adams, Hubbell [Edwin Powell Hubble] and Wecter."[66]

What Millikan opposed so vehemently was what he saw as the tendency toward "totalitarianism" and "the use of patronage to maintain the power of the group in control of the government."[67] The compromise bill (S. 1850) failed, much to the delight of even some of its nominal supporters in the science establishment. The National Science Foundation Act of 1950, finally enacted after a series of further compromises, established the foundation for the purpose of supporting basic research. Millikan was opposed to the end.

> So far as the science foundation bill is concerned, its worst feature inheres in the fact that it practically shuts the mouths of all of us scientists against opposing any kind of pressure group that is trying to get its feet in the federal trough. The aid to science that is now coming through defense organizations, whether it be army or navy, Atomic Energy Commission, Advisory Committee for Aeronautics, or other established government bureaus is practically free from politics in view of the fact research support is granted only to organizations that can demonstrate their capacity to solve the problems involved, rather than on the pork barrel basis. Since the main purpose of the federal government is national defense, it is altogether obvious that all the aid from the federal government that can possibly come under "the defense program" is legitimate.[68]

For Millikan, the defense departments alone were nonpolitical and outside the "pork barrel"; the federal government existed for defense and other functions were highly suspect. Millikan found few allies in this view of the federal government. The New Deal had made too many seemingly irreversible changes for that. Among scientists, Millikan and Jewett were for the most part isolated in their rejection of nonmilitary subsidy for research. They were lost in the surge toward broad-based governmental support. Their notion of "getting industry to support science in the universities as we tried to get them to do in the period 1928 to 1932" was hopelessly dated.[69]

Though Millikan would have been chagrined to see the growth of the dependence of the scientific community on federal funds, the defense-related agencies continued to provide—as he wished—the lion's share of support for research and development in America. According to National Science Foundation figures, federal expenditures on research and development in 1940 amounted to $74 million (about 0.8 percent of the total budget outlay); by 1949 the figure had already increased to $1.08 billion (2.7 percent of total outlays). Basic research was always dwarfed by applied research and development. But it should be noted that by 1955, after the establishment of the National Science Foundation, the Atomic Energy Commission and the Defense Department were the two largest "customers" for *basic* research alone. For fiscal 1960, the total federal budget obligations for research and development exceeded $8 billion more than $6 billion of which came from Defense and $425 million from the National Aeronautics and Space Administration. By 1963 obligations soared over $13.6 billion, with Defense providing $7.3 billion.[70]

To hindsight's eye, this growth of federal involvement seems inevitable and natural. The national government alone commands the resources to mount the increasingly expensive forays undertaken by Big Science. It should be noted, however, that a severe price has been exacted in return. As we near the end of the century, nostalgia for the days of unfettered, unbureaucratic science management is beginning to surface among many scientists. Whether such views will remain wishful thinking or enter the political arena remains to be determined. In any case, Millikan's opposition to uncritical acceptance of federal largess in the period 1946–50 was viewed at the time as weak and pitiable. This pioneer in American science was by then considered by many in the scientific community to be a relic of the past.[71]

When the *Autobiography of Robert A. Millikan* appeared in 1950, therefore, it was met in the scientific community with generous and thunderous platitudes. A grand old man had made his statement—a little rambling, a little unbalanced, but still a piece of Americana. There were no critical reviews. He had become, after all, a monument.

On scientific matters, Millikan was revered but not heeded. On social questions, the public looked, in that age of atomic anxiety, for calming reassurances about the future. Millikan was widely quoted on questions of science and religion, and on the stability of the world. A splendid but not atypical reaction to the *Autobiography* appeared in the *Cleveland News:* "ACE SCIENTIST IS SURE PLANET WILL STAY PUT."[72]

The project for this autobiography had begun much earlier. In 1939 Millikan had drafted handwritten memoirs titled "Scientific Recollections of Robert A. Millikan," comprising 214 small pages. The 1939 draft, along with articles and lectures composed during the 1930s and 1940s, ultimately were refashioned for the book that appeared in 1950.

In March 1946 Millikan had sent a copy of his autobiographical essay "Forks in the Road," prepared for an address before the Sunset Club in 1945, to the publishing house of Prentice-Hall. The essay delineated his good fortune to have been born just where, when, and who he was. The story line was a familiar one: by pluck and luck, Robert A. Millikan had made himself into a successful physicist. Prentice-Hall agreed to produce the book on receipt of an acceptable manuscript.

In June 1948 a large, rather unwieldy tome was delivered; Millikan explained his object to L. H. Christie of Prentice-Hall: "A professional biographer is obliged to paint the picture of his subject; the autobiographer must avoid that or else he violates every principle of good taste. The job I am trying to do is to paint the passing scene during the last eighty years as I have seen it."[73] The first draft, titled prosaically *Three Score Years and Twenty*, required cutting. After some minor wrangling about length, style, and substance, an agreeable draft was fashioned, and a second title, *Pioneering in Physics*, was suggested. The final title, *The Autobiography of Robert A. Millikan*, reflected the publisher's wishes more than Millikan's own. It is in a way a pity that the title *Pioneering in Physics* was not indeed selected, for it is far more expressive of the book's tone and substance than the one chosen.

The self-portrait that Millikan painted parallels closely the

Millikan reminisces. Courtesy of the Archives, California Institute of Technology.

familiar picture of the American pioneer. The pioneer came from wholesome stock. Heredity combined with environment to produce the beneficial result, for the pioneer found himself in the fortunate land. America proffered to him her rich fertile land to make of what he could. It was by devotion to duty, by hewing the virtuous path through the wilderness, that the pioneer would succeed. He was self-reliant, hard-working, and determined. He could expect little help, and despite the inevitable setbacks, his perseverance carried him to success. The story of the pioneers who overcame hardships to build the future is the mythic story Millikan retold in his *Autobiography*.

The first draft of the book began with a long chapter, "My Chromosomes," in which Millikan established his pioneer heritage. The chapter was overlong, and he agreed to drop it in favor of an introductory chapter of childhood reminiscences and recollections of his early education. His pioneer grandfather, Daniel Franklin Millikan, is the only forebear to be named; it was from Daniel, especially in the months he lived with him at age seven, that he received "an impressive object lesson in self-help," which above all else molded his character.[74]

He brought this "character" with him into the rich, fertile land of the new physics. Not only was the last third of the nineteenth century an exciting time for physics, but America itself was ripe for cultivation. During his lifetime, Millikan writes, "the United States was destined to rise from nowhere to a foremost place among the nations, not merely in material power, but also in *scientific*, as well as engineering, accomplishment."[75] How lucky he was, he recalls, to have been present at the creation of modern physics, in 1895–96, at the discovery of X rays, the electron, radioactivity, and a bit later the quantum and relativity!

In becoming a physicist, he had had encouragement—from Peck, from Pupin, from Michelson—but like the pioneers, he had not had help. His achievement was his own. Through long hours (at least a twelve-hour workday), through perseverance, through determination, he made himself into a successful physicist. Like the pioneers, too, he had had setbacks and disappointments. It was not, after all, until he was over forty that success in research was his. Millikan's *Autobiography* confirms Alfred Kazin's wise perception that "every American story revolving around the self... is a story of making it against a background symbolically American."[76]

The success he sought was complex. Though he enjoyed the company of the rich and famous, and though he did not shun material success, he did not define his achievements in terms of wealth and position. Although he enjoyed and took considerable (some say overweening) pride in his honors and medals, they do not exhaust his understanding of success. He yearned throughout his life to make an *enduring* contribution to science. For him the goal was Truth, durable, unwavering Truth, in which he could have his portion. He measured himself in these terms, and it comes as no surprise to see how jealously he guarded his contributions, and how personally vulnerable he felt when new experiments were hailed as superseding his own.

In so many ways, Millikan conforms to the general pattern of the self-made man noted by several authors. The feelings of inadequacy that we have seen plagued him all his life were appeased by his efforts at proving his importance—to others, but mainly to himself. His identity was wrapped up in his achievements. Attacks on his science were converted by him into assaults on his *self*.[77] But like all self-made men, he saw himself as overcoming hardships to build the future. "Each new theory is built like a cathedral through the addition of many builders of many different elements."[78] He wrote near the close of the *Autobiography:*

> I took credit for a few wise decisions myself, and why not, for while the Great Architect had to direct alone the earlier stages of the evolutionary process, that part of Him that becomes us...has been stepping up amazingly the *pace* of...evolution since we began to become conscious of the part we had to play. *It is our sense of responsibility for playing our part to the best of our ability that makes us Godlike.*[79]

Just as revealing as the pioneer image he wished to project are the *Autobiography*'s omissions. Absent from the account are the missteps, the errors of judgment, and problem choices. Millikan's physics career assumes a new aspect: one of unfailing insight and unilinear contribution. The early photoelectric work, which had begun as an attempt to resolve differences in J. J. Thomson's and Philipp Lenard's formulations of the electron theory of metals, was recast as a simple determination of a simple fact: whether the effects increase with rising temperature. The only theoretical discussion involved Einstein's work, which in fact had been ignored in Millikan's early work.[80] Similarly, the second-phase photoelectric work is discussed—amazingly—in a chapter titled "The Experimental Proof of the Existence of the Photon—Einstein's Photoelectric Equation." When he wrote, "I thought that the emitted electron that escapes with the energy hv gets that energy by the direct transfer of hv units of energy from the light to the electron and hence scarcely permits of any other interpretation than that which Einstein had originally suggested, namely that of the semi-corpuscular or photon theory of light itself,"[81] he was deceiving himself. He remained, readers may remember, an opponent of the photon theory for years after his work on Einstein's equation.

Millikan's years devoted to cosmic ray research received scant attention in the *Autobiography*. The atom-building hypothesis and its atom-annihilation successors, which had been major motivating forces in his intellectual life for so long, are omitted entirely. Their dénouement had come in fact only in the year of the *Autobiography*'s appearance. A note inked in on a reprint of his article on cosmic rays for the *Reviews of Modern Physics* in 1949 confessed his final, reluctant abandonment of his latest cherished hypothesis: "New evidence has appeared since this was written, which is unfavorable to this hypothesis, but the experimental data contained herein is valid. The actual origin of the cosmic rays is still today an unsolved mystery."[82]

After the appearance of the *Autobiography* and its generally predictable acceptance, the infirmities of age took a heavier and heavier toll on Millikan. He was hospitalized in September 1953 and then entered a convalescent home in Pasadena, where he died December 19, 1953. His body was removed to the Memorial Court of Honor of the Great Mausoleum at Forest Lawn Memorial Park, where it lay in state until the funeral.[83]

Millikan received many eulogies from those who knew him or were touched by his example all over the world. No tribute would have pleased him more than that by his Caltech colleague Lee Dubridge:

[Millikan] left to the world a three-fold monument: his imperishable contributions to knowledge, his creation in Caltech of a new kind of scientific institution, and the inspiration he gave to hundreds of students. The scientific community in America "grew up" between 1915 and 1940. It would be hard to find a man who contributed more to this maturing process than Robert A. Millikan.[84]

For us, however, the scientific *éloge* ought no longer to serve merely as a tribute. We are obliged to remind ourselves that for our age Millikan is no sage. The verities that he grasped so securely were never quite so simple as he perceived them to be. Millikan "saw" the triumph of science and scientific method as clearly as he "saw" his electrons leaping to and from his oil drops. The era in which Millikan could claim that "the supreme question for all mankind is how it can best stimulate and accelerate the applications of the scientific method to all departments of human life" has passed.[85]

Bibliographical Note

A. Manuscript Resources

For this study I have drawn extensively on a number of manuscript collections. By far the most important are those deposited at the California Institute of Technology: the Robert A. Millikan Papers, the George Ellery Hale Papers, and the papers of Edward Barrett, James Scherer, Arthur Amos Noyes, Arthur Fleming, Paul Epstein, and Ira Sprague Bowen. Other collections of note include the Gilbert Newton Lewis Papers and the Ernest Orlando Lawrence Papers (University of California, Berkeley); the Henry Crew Papers (Niels Bohr Library, American Institute of Physics); the P. M. S. Blackett Papers (the Royal Society, London); the Sir Joseph John Thomson Papers (Cambridge University Library); the John Campbell Merriam Papers (Library of Congress); the Arthur H. Compton Papers (Washington University, St. Louis); the Millikan file, Oberlin College Archives; the William Welch Papers (Johns Hopkins University); and the Ogden Nicholas Rood Papers (Columbia University).

B. Published Sources

The basic published source on Robert Millikan is his own *Autobiography of Robert A. Millikan* (New York, 1950), but it must be used with care. Other valuable accounts include Lee A. Dubridge and Paul Epstein, "Robert Andrews Millikan," in *National Academy of Sciences Biographical Memoirs* 33 (1959):241–82; Paul Epstein, "Robert A. Millikan as Physicist and Teacher," *Reviews of Modern Physics* 20 (1948):10–25; Daniel Kevles, "Robert Andrews Millikan," *Dictionary of Scientific Biography;* Kevles, "Millikan: Spokesman for Science in the Twenties," *Engineering and Science* 32 (April 1969):17–22; Robert Kargon, "The Conservative Mode: Robert A. Millikan and the Twentieth Century Revolution in Physics," *Isis* 88 (1977):590–26, and "Birth Cries of the Elements," in *The Analytic Spirit,* ed. Harry Woolf (Ithica, 1981), pp 309–25; and Gerald Holton, "Subelectrons, Presuppositions, and the Millikan-Ehrenhaft Debate," *Historical Studies in the Physical Sciences* 9 (1978):161–224. Jesse W. M. Du Mond's introduction to the reprint of Millikan's 1917 classic contains valuable personal insights: "Editor's Introduction" in Robert A. Millikan, *The Electron* (Chicago, 1917/1968), pp. xi–lvii. Alfred Romer's excellent article "Robert A. Millikan, Physics Teacher," *Physics Teacher* (February 1978):78–85, deserves special mention.

On American physics during Millikan's active years, the most comprehensive treatment is Daniel Kevles' *The Physicists: The History of a Scientific Community in Modern America* (New York, 1978), which includes a splendid bibliography. Other useful works include Dorothy Michelson Livingston, *The Master of Light: A Biography of Albert A. Michelson* (New York, 1973); Loyd Swenson, "Albert A. Michelson," *Dictionary of Scientific Biography;* Roger Stuewer, *The Compton Effect* (New York, 1975) and "Non-Einsteinian Interpretations of the Photoelectric Effect," in *Historical and Philosophical Perspectives on Science,* ed. Roger Stuewer (Minneapolis, 1970); Stanley Coben, "The Scientific Establishment and the Transmission of Quantum Mechanics to the United States, 1919–1932," *American Historical Review* 76 (1971):442–66; J. H. Van Vleck, "American Physics Comes of Age," *Physics Today* 17 (1964):21–26; Spencer Weart, "The Physics Business in America, 1919–1940," in *The Sciences in the American Context,* ed. Nathan Reingold (Washington, D.C., 1979), pp. 295–358; Charles Weiner, "A New Site for the Seminar: The Refugees and American Physics in the Thirties," in *The Intellectual Migration,* ed. Donald Fleming and Bernard Bailyn (Cambridge, Mass., 1969), pp. 190–234; Lawrence Badash, *Radioactivity in America: Growth and Decay of a Science* (Baltimore, 1979); and Charles Weiner, "Moving into the New Physics," *Physics Today* 25 (May 1972):40–49.

There is no single good comprehensive treatment of American science generally during this period. Recent collections that may profitably be consulted are Nathan Reingold, ed., *The Sciences in the American Context* (Washington, D.C., 1978), and Alexandra Oleson and John Voss, eds., *The Organization of Knowledge in Modern America, 1860–1920* (Baltimore, 1979). A key figure during this time has found a fine biographer in Helen Wright, *Explorer of the Universe: A Biography of George Ellery Hale* (New York, 1966). Other sources that may usefully be consulted include Ronald Tobey, *The American Ideology of National Science, 1919–1930* (Pittsburgh, 1971); Daniel Kevles, "George Ellery Hale, the First World War, and the Advancement of Science in America," *Isis* 59 (1968):427–37; Robert Kargon, ed., *The Maturing of American Science* (Washington, D.C., 1974); A. Hunter Dupree, *Science in the Federal Government* (Cambridge, Mass., 1957); Lawrence Veysey, *The Emergence of the American University* (Chicago, 1965); and Charles Rosenberg, *No Other Gods: On Science and American Social Thought* (Baltimore, 1976).

Abbreviations

Akad. Wetensch. Amst. Proc.	*Akademie van Wetenschappen, Amsterdam, Proceedings*
Akad. Wiss. Wien Ber.	*Akademie der Wissenschaften, Wien, Berichte*
Amer. Jour. Phys.	*American Journal of Physics*
Amer. Jour. Psych.	*American Journal of Psychology*
Amer. Jour. Sci.	*American Journal of Science*
Amer. Quart.	*American Quarterly*
Ann. Phys. & Chem.	*Annalen der Physik und Chemie*
Ann. Physik	*Annalen der Physik*
Ann. physique	*Annales de physique*
Astro. Jour.	*Astronomical Journal*
Astron. & Astrophys.	*Astronomy and Astrophysics*
Astrophys. Jour.	*Astrophysical Journal*
BAAS Rpts.	*Reports of the British Association for the Advancement of Science*
Biog. Mem. Nat. Acad. Sci.	*Biographical Memoirs of the National Academy of Sciences*
Bull. Cal. Inst. Tech.	*Bulletin of the California Institute of Technology*
CIW Rpts.	*Reports of the Carnegie Institution of Washington*
CIW Yrbk.	*Yearbook of the Carnegie Institution of Washington*
Comptes rendus	*Comptes rendus hebdomadaires des séances de l'Académie des Sciences*
DSB	*Dictionary of Scientific Biography*
GEH	**George Ellery Hale Papers, California Institute of Technology, Pasadena**
Hist. Stud. Phys. Sci.	*Historical Studies in the Physical Sciences*
Jour. Amer. Inst. Elect. Eng.	*Journal of the American Institute of Electrical Engineers*
Jour. Chem. Soc.	*Journal of the Chemical Society*
Jour. Franklin Inst.	*Journal of the Franklin Institute*

Abbreviations

Nat. Acad. Sci. Biog. Mem.	National Academy of Sciences Biographical Memoirs
OCA	Oberlin College Archives
Phil. Mag.	Philosophical Magazine
Phil. Trans.	Philosophical Transactions of the Royal Society of London
Phys. Rev.	Physical Review
Phys. Zeits.	Physikalische Zeitschrift
Pogg. Ann.	Poggendorff's Annalen der Physik
Pop. Sci. Mon.	Popular Science Monthly
Proc. Amer. Phil. Soc.	Proceedings of the American Philosophical Society
Proc. Camb. Phil. Soc.	Proceedings of the Cambridge Philosophical Society
Proc. Leeds Phil. & Lit. Soc.	Proceedings of the Leeds Philosophical and Literary Society
Proc. Nat. Acad. Sci.	Proceedings of the National Academy of Sciences
Proc. Roy. Soc.	Proceedings of the Royal Society of London
Publ. Astr. Soc. Pac.	Publications of the Astronomical Society of the Pacific
RAM	Robert A. Millikan Papers, California Institute of Technology, Pasadena
Rev. Mod. Phys.	Reviews of Modern Physics
Rev. Sci. Inst.	Review of Scientific Instruments
Sci. Amer.	Scientific American
Smith. Inst. Ann. Rpt.	Annual Report of the Smithsonian Institution
Tokyo Inst. Phys. & Chem. Res. Rpts.	Tokyo Institute of Physical and Chemical Research Reports
Trans. Kans. Acad. Sci.	Transactions of the Kansas Academy of Science
Trans. N.Y. Acad. Sci.	Transactions of the New York Academy of Sciences
Verh. D. phys. Gesell.	Verhandlungen der Deutsche physikalische Gesellschaft
Zeits. Astrophys.	Zeitschrift für Astrophysik
Zeits. phys. Chem.	Zeitschrift für physikalische Chemie

Notes

1. A Brief Introduction

1. Arthur D. Little, "Physics and Civilization," *Atlantic Monthly* 134 (1924):36.
2. William Leuchtenburg, *The Perils of Prosperity, 1914–1932* (Chicago, 1958), pp. 178–232.
3. Herbert Hoover, "The Nation and Science," *Science* 65 (1927):27.
4. Robert Millikan, *Science* 59 (1924):10.
5. Millikan, *Science* 58 (1923):296.
6. Simon Newcomb, "Exact Science in America," *North American Review* 119 (1874):286, 307.
7. J. M. Mackie, *From Cape Cod to Dixie and the Tropics* (New York, 1864), pp. 200–201.
8. Harold Vatter, *The Drive to Industrial Maturity* (Westport, Conn., 1975), chap. 3.
9. John Kenneth Galbraith, *The New Industrial State* (New York, 1967), p. 82.
10. Robert Wiebe, *The Search for Order* (New York, 1967), pp. 111–32.
11. Ibid., p. 147.
12. *World's Work* 49 (1925):242.
13. Lawrence Veysey, *The Emergence of the American University* (Chicago, 1965); Hugh Hawkins, *Pioneer* (Ithaca, 1960) and *Between Harvard and America* (New York, 1972); Burton Bledstein, *The Culture of Professionalism* (New York, 1976); Robert Storr, *The Beginning of the Future* (New York, 1973).
14. William W. Folwell, *University Addresses* (Minneapolis, 1909), pp. 17–18.
15. Robert Millikan, "New Truth and Old," *Bull. Cal. Inst. Tech.* 35 (1926):9–10.
16. *New York Times*, May 7, 1950, sec. 7, p. 1.
17. *New York Times*, December 20, 1953, p. 1.

2. The Making of a Scientist

1. A. T. Andreas, *Illustrated Historical Atlas of Iowa* (Chicago, 1875), pp. 443–44.

2. Robert A. Millikan, *The Autobiography of Robert A. Millikan* (New York, 1950), pp. 5–6.

3. F. I. Kuhns, "Congregational Christians in Iowa," *Palimpsest* 32 (1951):197.

4. William Peterson. *The Story of Iowa* (New York, 1952), 2:685–87.

5. Robert A. Millikan, "Eugenics Record Office Form," December 31, 1926, RAM 68.7, 68.8.

6. Ibid.

7. Interview with Millikan, *Los Angeles Times,* July 21, 1929, RAM 68.1.

8. "Juvenilia," p. 3, RAM.

9. "Autobiographical Notes," RAM 67.7, 68.2. On the self-made man, see Irvin Wyllie, *The Self-Made Man in America* (New Brunswick, N.J., 1954).

10. Robert A. Millikan to Max Millikan, May 27, 1944, RAM 58.10.

11. Robert A. Millikan to Glenn Millikan, April 24, 1928, RAM 58.5.

12. "Juvenilia," RAM.

13. Statement of R. A. Millikan, May 3, 1935, OCA.

14. List of courses, OCA.

15. "Scientific Recollections of R. A. Millikan" (1939), RAM 67.3–67.6.

16. Oberlin College catalogue, 1891–92, p. 50, and 1892–93, p. 58, OCA.

17. Robert A. Millikan to Glenn Millikan, April 24, 1928, RAM 57.5.

18. Leonard S. Reich, "The Structure of American Physics, 1876–1916: A Computer-Assisted Study," unpublished seminar paper, Johns Hopkins University, 1974, pp. 38–45. After examining the records of the universities, I have revised Reich's figures slightly upward.

19. Lawrence Veysey, *The Emergence of the American University* (Chicago, 1965), pp. 21–56.

20. Quoted in ibid., p. 33.

21. Quoted in ibid. p. 161.

22. Henry Rowland, "The Physical Laboratory in Modern Education," in *The Physical Papers of Henry Augustus Rowland* (Baltimore, 1902), pp. 617–18.

23. Rutherford to J. J. Thomson, December 26, 1902, Sir J. J. Thomson Papers, Cambridge University Library.

24. Millikan, *Autobiography,* p. 18. Dorothy Michelson Livingston provides a strikingly different picture of Rood in *The Master of Light: A Biography of Albert A. Michelson* (New York, 1973), p. 187.

25. Edward L. Nichols, "Ogden Nicholas Rood," *Nat. Acad. Sci. Biog. Mem.* 6(1909):449–72; Daniel Kevles, "Ogden Nicholas Rood," *DSB* 11:531–32. Rood's papers are at the Butler Library, Columbia University.

26. *American Men of Science,* 1906, p. 133.

27. Columbia College, *University Bulletin,* no. 6 (1893), p. 27; no. 7 (1894), pp. 44–45; no. 10 (1895), pp. 36–37; no. 12 (1895), pp. 40–45.

28. Robert A. Millikan to Glenn Millikan, April 24, 1928, RAM 57.5.

29. Livingston, *Master of Light,* p. 186; Daniel Kevles, "Albert Abraham Michelson," *DSB* 9:395–400.

30. On these measurements see Kevles, "Albert Abraham Michelson"; Bernard Jaffe, *Michelson and the Speed of Light* (Garden City, N.Y., 1960), pp. 49–57, 111–23.

31. *Nobel Lectures: Physics 1901–1921* (Amsterdam, 1967), p. 164.

32. Millikan, *Autobiography,* p. 23.

33. Albert A. Michelson, "Some of the Objects and Methods of Physical Science," *Quarterly Calendar* 6 (August 1894):15.

34. Robert Millikan, "Albert Abraham Michelson, 1852–1931," *Nat. Acad. Sci. Biog. Mem.* 19 (1938):124–25.

35. Millikan, "Scientific Recollections," RAM 67.3, pp. 19–20; "Autobiographical Notes," RAM 67.7.

36. *Trans. N.Y. Acad. Sci.* 14 (1895):155–85; *Phys. Rev.* 3 (1895):81–99, 177–92. A similar study by W. von Uljonin of Moscow appeared later in *Ann. Phys. & Chem.* 62 (1897):528–42.

37. Millikan, *Autobiography,* pp. 26–29. See also "Scientific Recollections" (1939), RAM 67.3–67.6.

38. Walther Nernst, *Zeits, phys. Chem.* 14 (1894):622–26.

39. Robert A. Millikan, "Eine experimentelle Prüfung der Clausius-Mossotti'schen Formel," *Ann. Phys. & Chem.* 60 (1897):376–80. A fuller discussion of this paper and of a reported theoretical part can be found in Paul Epstein, "Robert Andrews Millikan as Physicist and Teacher," *Rev. Mod. Phys.* 20 (1948):11.

40. Millikan, *Autobiography,* p. 58.

41. Millikan to William Rainey Harper, September 22, 1896, RAM 43.11; original in Presidential Papers, 1889–1925, University of Chicago.

42. James Clerk Maxwell, *Scientific Papers,* ed. W. D. Niven (New York, 1965), 2:243.

43. Michelson, "Some of the Objects," p. 15.

44. Millikan, "Albert Abraham Michelson," p. 122.

3. The Scientist as Investigator

1. Robert A. Millikan, *Autobiography of Robert A. Millikan* (New York, 1950), p. 37.

2. Albert A. Michelson, "Some of the Objects and Methods of Physical Science," *Quarterly Calendar* 6 (August 1894):15.

3. See Lawrence Badash, "The Completeness of Nineteenth-Century Science," *Isis* 63 (1972):52.

4. Quoted in Dorothy Michelson Livingston, *The Master of Light: A Biography of Albert A. Michelson* (New York, 1973), p. 190.

Notes

5. Albert A. Michelson, "A Theory of X-Rays," *Amer. Jour. Sci.* 1 (1896):312–15; Michelson and S. W. Stratton, "The Source of X-Rays," *Science* 3 (1896):694–97.

6. Richard Storr, *Harper's University: The Beginnings* (Chicago, 1966), p. 211.

7. University of Chicago, *Annual Register, 1898–1899,* p. 129.

8. Storr, *Harper's University,* pp. 212–13.

9. University of Chicago, *President's Report, 1898–1899,* p. xi.

10. Ibid., p. xiii.

11. Millikan, *Autobiography,* pp. 42–44.

12. *Phy. Rev.* 6 (1898):1–17.

13. *Phys. Rev.* 5 (1897):231–46.

14. *Phil. Mag.* 47 (1899):501–22.

15. *Phys. Rev.* 14 (1902):1–16.

16. Millikan, "Albert Abraham Michelson," in *Biog. Mem. Nat. Acad. Sci.* 19 (1938):126.

17. Chicago, 1898.

18. University of Chicago, *President's Report, 1898–1899,* p. 66.

19. Millikan to William Rainey Harper, April 12, 1898, RAM 43.11; originals at the University of Chicago.

20. Millikan, *Autobiography,* p. 48.

21. University of Chicago, *President's Report, 1898–1899,* p. 181.

22. Millikan, *Autobiography,* p. 59.

23. Millikan, "Some Episodes in the Scientific Work of Robert A. Millikan," RAM 67.8.

24. J. J. Thomson, "The Roentgen Rays," *Nature* 53 (1896):392.

25. J. J. Thomson, *The Discharge of Electricity through Gases* (Westminster, 1898), pp. 4–5.

26. Rutherford, *Phil. Mag.* 134 (1899):109.

27. Alexander Finlay, *A Hundred Years of Chemistry* (London, 1948), pp. 203–5.

28. RAM 3.8.

29. Millikan, *Autobiography,* p. 50.

30. "Lecture Notes on Radioactivity," RAM 1.8.

31. RAM 1.4, 1.9, 1.10.

32. Millikan, "Recent Discoveries in Radiation and Their Significance," *Pop. Sci. Mon.* 64 (1904):492.

33. Ibid., p. 498. See also Millikan, "Radium: The Revolutionary Element," *Technical World* 1 (1904):1–10.

34. Millikan, "Recent Discoveries," pp. 496–97. See also Lawrence Badash, *Rutherford and Boltwood* (New Haven, 1969), p. 57n.

35. Millikan, "Recent Discoveries," p. 498.

36. Ibid. For similar views, see Frederick Soddy, "Radioactivity," *Electrician* 52 (1904):725.

37. University of Chicago, *President's Report, 1902–1904,* p. 216.

38. Millikan, "The Relation between the Radioactivity and the Uranium Content of Certain Minerals," in *Congress of Arts and Sciences*

Universal Exposition, St. Louis, 1904 ed. Howard Rogers (Boston, 1906), 4:187. See also Lawrence Badash, *Radioactivity in America* (Baltimore, 1979), pp. 78–80.

39. I am indebted for much of the information in this paragraph to helpful discussion with Lawrence Badash.

40. *Phil. Mag.* 1 (1901):147–59.

41. *Phil. Mag.* 9 (1905):692–706.

42. *Phil. Mag.* 10 (1905): 617–31.

43. Millikan, *Autobiography,* p. 61.

44. Hobbs, *Phil. Mag.* 10 (1905):619, 631.

45. N. R. Campbell, *Phil. Mag.* 9 (1905):531–44; J. J. Thomson, *Phil. Mag.* 10 (1905):584–90; Ernest Rutherford, "Present Problems of Radioactivity," in *Congress of Arts and Sciences,* ed. Rogers, 4:186.

46. Wilhelm Weber, *Pogg. Ann.* 156 (1875):1.

47. *Ann. Phys. & Chem.* 66 (1898):545–81.

48. Paul Drude, *Ann. Phys. & Chem.* 1 (1900):566–613. On Riecke and Drude, see E. T. Whitaker, *History of the Theories of Aether and Electricity* (New York, 1960), 1:418–20; A. H. Wilson, *The Theory of Metals* (Cambridge, 1936), pp. 1–2. See also the articles on Riecke and Drude by Stanley Goldberg in *DSB.* These ideas were developed more fully in H. A. Lorentz, *Theory of Electrons* (New York, 1915/1952), pp. 10, 63–65.

49. Wilhelm Hallwachs, *Ann. Phys.* 33 (1888):301–12.

50. Philipp Lenard, *Ann. Physik* 2 (1900):359–75; J. J. Thomson, *Phil. Mag.* 48 (1899), p. 547.

51. H. S. Allen, *Photoelectricity* (London 1913), pp. 1–13.

52. J. J. Thomson, *The Conduction of Electricity through Gases* (Cambridge, 1903), p. 241.

53. Lenard, *Ann. Physik* 2 (1900): 374–75, 8 (1902):194–98. See Bruce Wheaton, *Hist. Stud. Phys. Sci.* 9 (1978):299–322.

54. Millikan and George Winchester, *Phil. Mag.* 14 (1907):188. Millikan was engaged as well in exploring other aspects of the kinetic theory of metals. He directed his student Newland F. Smith to the problem of the effect of tension in wires on thermal and electrical conductivity; Smith wrote, "The development of the electron theory of metallic conduction has given new interest to measurements of thermal and electrical conductivity;; (*Phys. Rev.* 28 [1909]:107).

55. George Winchester, *Phys. Rev.* 25 (1907):103–14.

56. Millikan and Winchester, *Phil. Mag.* 14 (1907):191, 210; emphasis mine.

57. See, for example, A. Lienhop, *Ann. Phys.* 21 (1906):281–304; H. Dember, *Ann. Phys.* 23 (1907):957–62.

58. Millikan, *Autobiography,* p. 61.

59. Ibid., pp. 68–69.

60. Ibid., p. 69.

61. University of Chicago, *Annual Register, 1898–1899,* p. 297.

62. *Phil. Mag.* 19 (1910):209.

63. See David Anderson, *The Discovery of the Electron* (Princeton,

1964), pp. 74–80; Daniel Kevles, "Robert Andrews Millikan, *DSB;* Paul Epstein, "Robert Andrews Millikan as Physicist and Teacher," *Rev. Mod. Phys.* 20 (1948):10–25; Robert Millikan, *The Electron* (Chicago, 1917), pp. 43–63; Alfred Romer, "The Experimental History of Atomic Charges, 1895–1903," *Isis* 34 (1942):150–61.

64. J. J. Thomson, *Phil. Mag.* 46 (1898):528, 48 (1899):547, 5 (1903):346; C. T. R. Wilson, *Camb. Phil. Soc. Proc.* (1897):333.

65. J. J. Thomson, *Phil. Mag.* 48 (1899):561.

66. H. A. Wilson, *Phil. Mag.* 5 (1903):430.

67. Ibid., p. 434.

68. Millikan, *Electron*, p. 54.

69. Wilson, *Phil. Mag.* 5 (1903):434–35.

70. J. J. Thomson, *Electricity and Matter* (New York, 1904), pp. 72–83.

71. Millikan and Begeman, *Phys. Rev.* 26 (1908):197–99.

72. Begeman, *Phys. Rev.* 31 (1910):45.

73. The expression is: $q = 3.422 \times 10^{-9} \frac{g}{E} V_g^{3/2}$, where V_g is the rate of fall, g is the acceleration due to gravity, and E is the field strength.

74. Millikan, *Phil. Mag.* 19 (1910):209–28, esp. p. 223.

75. Millikan, *Phys. Rev.* 32 (1911):387.

76. Millikan, *Autobiography*, p. 75.

77. Millikan, *Science* 32 (1910:436.

78. Millikan, *Autobiography*, p. 75.

79. $\Delta q = \frac{mg}{XV_g} \Delta V_x$

80. Millikan, *Phys. Rev.* 32 (1911):349–97.

81. Ibid., pp. 349–97; Millikan, *Phys. Rev.* 2 (1913):109–43 and *Phil. Mag.* 34 (1917):1–30.

82. See Gerald Holton, "Subelectrons, Presuppositions, and the Millikan-Ehrenhaft Dispute," *Hist. Stud. Phys. Sci.* 9 (1978):161–224.

83. Millikan, *Electron*, p. 70.

84. Millikan, *Autobiography*, p. 82.

85. Millikan, "Atomic Theories of Radiation," *Science* 37 (1913)133, and "A Direct Photoelectric Determination of Planck's 'h,'" *Phys. Rev.* 7 (1916):355.

86. "Scientific Recollections," RAM 67.3, pp. 56–57.

87. Ibid., p. 59.

88. Millikan, "Some New Values of the Positive Potentials Assumed by Metals in a High Vacuum under the Influence of Ultra-Violet Light," *Phys. Rev.* 30 (1910):287–88.

89. Millikan, "The Effect of the Character of the Source upon the Velocities of Emission of Electrons Liberated by Ultra Violet Light," *Phys. Rev.* 35 (1912):74–76.

90. Millikan, "On the Cause of the Apparent Differences between Spark and Arc Sources in One Imparting of Initial Speeds to Photoelectrons," *Phys. Rev.* 1 (1913):73–75. See also the criticism of Robert Pohl and Peter Pringsheim in *Verh. D. Phys. Gesell.* 14 (1912):974–82.

91. Millikan, *Autobiography,* p. 94.

92. Rudolf Ladenburg, *Phys. Zeit.* 8 (1907):590–94; Jakob Kunz, *Phys. Rev.* 29 (1909):3 and 30 (1909):212; David Cornelius, *Phys. Rev.* 1 (1913: 16.

93. O. W. Richardson, *Phys. Rev.* 34 (1912):146–49 and *Science* 36 (1912): 57–58; Richardson and K. T. Compton, *Phil. Mag.* 24 (1912):575.

94. A. L. Hughes, *Phil. Trans.* 212 (1912): 205–26.

95. Pohl and Pringsheim, *Verh. D. phys. Gesell.* 15 (1913):637.

96. Pohl and Pringsheim, *Verh. D. phys. Gesell.* 14 (1912):974–82.

97. Millikan, *Phys. Rev.* 1 (1913):73–75. See also Roger Stuewer, *The Compton Effect* (New York, 1975), pp. 72–73.

98. William Kadesch, "Energy of Photo-Electrons from Sodium and Potassium as a Function of the Frequency of the Incident Light," *Phys. Rev.* 3 (1914):367.

99. Hughes, *Proc. Camb. Phil. Soc.* 16 (1911):167–74.

100. Kadesch. *Phys. Rev.* 3 (1914):367–74.

101. Millikan, "A Direct Determination of 'h,'" *Phys. Rev.* 4 (1914): 73–75.

102. Millikan, *Phys. Rev.* 7 (1916):355–87.

103. Millikan, "Quantum Relations in Photo-electric Phenomena," *Proc. Nat. Acad. Sci.* 2 (1916):78.

104. Ibid., p. 83.

105. Millikan, *Phys. Rev.* 7 (1916):384.

106. Millikan, *Electron,* p. 230.

107. Ibid., p. 230.

108. Stuewer, *Compton Effect,* p. 88n.

109. Millikan, "Quantum Relations in Photo-electric Phenomena," *Proc. Nat. Acad. Sci.* 2 (1916):83.

110. *Nobel Lectures: Physics, 1922–1931* (Amsterdam, 1965), p. 51.

111. Millikan, *Phys. Rev.* 7 (1916):357–59.

112. Epstein, "Robert Andrews Millikan as Physicist," p. 12.

113. *Nobel Lectures,* p. 56.

114. Millikan, "New Proofs of the Kinetic Theory of Matter and the Atomic Theory of Electricity," *Pop. Sci. Mon.* 80 (1912):417–19.

115. Millikan, "Twentieth-Century Physics," *Smith. Inst. Ann. Rpt., 1918* (Washington, D.C., 1920), pp. 171, 175.

116. Millikan, *Electron,* p. 5.

117. Robert Multhauf, "The Society and Its Concerns," *Isis* 66 (1975):455.

118. Millikan, *Autobiography,* p. 44. Also see Duane Roller, "Millikan's Influence," *Rev. Mod. Phys.* 20 (1948):26–30.

119. Frank B. Jewett to Millikan, October 31, 1923, RAM 40.25.

120. P. W. Bridgman, *Science* 112 (1950):316.

121. J. P. Guilford, "Three Faces of Intellect," *Amer. Jour. Psych.* 14 (1959):470, and *The Nature of Human Intelligence* (New York, 1967), p. 171.

122. Millikan, "Scientific Recollections," p. 96.

123. Millikan, "Some Exceptional Opportunities in Southern California," RAM 27.9, pp. 1, 2, 5. In all fairness it must be admitted that, like many of his contemporaries, Millikan thought in terms of social stereotypes, but his personal behavior toward members of non-Anglo-Saxon groups was fair and decent.

124. Millikan to Amos Miller, June 6, 1942, RAM 14.20. I am grateful to Clayton Koppes for this reference.

125. J. W. Getzels and P. W. Jackson, "The Highly Intelligent and the Highly Creative Adolescent," in *Scientific Creativity: Its Recognition and Development*, ed. C. Taylor and F. Barron (New York, 1966), p. 172.

126. Thomas Kuhn, "The Essential Tension: Tradition and Innovation in Scientific Research," in *Scientific Creativity*, ed. Taylor and Barron, p. 342.

127. Ibid., p. 352.

128. Bridgman, *Science* 112 (1950):316.

129. *Nobel Lectures: Physics, 1901–1921* (Amsterdam, 1967), p. 480.

130. *Nobel Lectures: Physics, 1922–1941* (Amsterdam, 1965), p. 53.

131. Ibid., p. 65.

132. A. H. Compton, *Proc. Nat. Acad. Sci.* 9 (1923):359; J. A. Becker, E. C. Watson, and W. R. Smythe, *Phys. Rev.* 23 (1924):89.

133. Epstein and Ehrenfest, *Proc. Nat. Acad. Sci.* 10 (1924), p. 133.

134. Millikan, *Jour. Chem. Soc.* 125 (1924):1416–17.

135. *Nobel Lectures: Physics, 1922–1941*, p. 54.

136. Millikan, "Evolution vs. Revolution," *Bull. Cal. Inst. Tech.* 51 (1942):6–7.

4. The Scientist in Action

1. George Ellery Hale to Millikan, August 31, 1897, RAM 4.15.

2. Robert A. Millikan to Greta Millikan, July 19, 1916, RAM 53.

3. Hale to James Scherer, May 30, 1916, James Scherer Papers, California Institute of Technology, Box 2, folder 6.

4. Millikan, *The Autobiography of Robert A. Millikan* (New York, 1950), pp. 129–30; RAM 67.3-67.6, p. 116.

5. Robert A. Millikan to Greta Millikan, July 19, 1916, RAM 53.

6. G. E. Hale, "National Academies and the Progress of Research II," *Science* 39 (1914):199.

7. Hale to William H. Welch, July 13, 1915, William Welch Papers, Johns Hopkins University, Box 35.

8. Welch to Hale, July 14, 1915, Welch Papers, Box 35.

9. L. N. Scott, *The Naval Consulting Board of the United States* (Washington, D.C., 1920), pp. 10–11.

10. Hale to Welch, July 13, 1915, Welch Papers, Box 35.

11. See G. E. Hale, "The National Research Council," in *The New World of Science: Its Development during the War*, ed. Robert M. Yerkes

(New York, 1920), pp. 13–30; Daniel Kevles, "George Ellery Hale, the First World War, and the Advancement of Science in America," *Isis* 59 (1968):430–32.

12. G. E. Hale, "National Academies and the Progress of Research," *Science*38 (1913):680–82.

13. *Science* 43 (1916):766.

14. National Research Council, *Third Annual Report* (Washington, D.C., 1919), p. 26; Kevles, "George Ellery Hale," p. 432.

15. Robert A. Millikan to Greta Millikan, April 1, 1917, RAM 53.1.

16. Daniel Kevles, *The Physicists* (New York, 1978), p. 133, and "Robert Andrews Millikan," *DSB* 9:395–400.

17. I. B. Cohen, "American Physicists at War: From the First World War to 1942," *Amer. Jour. Phys.* 13 (1945):333–46; Millikan, *Autobiography*, pp. 157–80. See also Kevles' excellent discussion in *The Physicists*, chap. 9.

18. *Autobiography, pp. 176–77.*

19. Hale, "Introduction," in New World of Science, ed. Yerkes, pp. vii–xiv.

20. Millikan, "The New Opportunity in Science," *Science* 50 (1919): 285.

21. Yerkes, ed., *New World of Science*, pp. 39–48.

22. Millikan, "New Opportunity," pp. 289–90 and "Some Scientific Aspects of the Meteorological Work of the United States Army," in *New World of Science*, ed. Yerkes, pp. 49–62.

23. C. J. West, "The Chemical Warfare Service," in *New World of Science*, ed. Yerkes, p. 153.

24. Millikan, "New Opportunity," p. 291.

25. Ibid., p. 292.

26. See, for example, C. Rosenberg, "Science and American Social Thought," in *Science and Society in the United States*, ed. David van Tassel and Michael Hall (Homewood, Ill., 1966), pp. 135–62; Edwin Layton, *The Revolt of the Engineers* (Cleveland, 1971), chap. 3; Robert Wiebe, *The Search for Order* (New York, 1968), chap. 6.

27. See John Kenneth Galbraith, *The New Industrial State* (Boston, 1967), chap. 6.

28. Millikan, "New Opportunity," p. 293–94.

29. Ibid., p. 296.

30. Ibid., p. 297.

31. Kevles, "George Ellery Hale," p. 437.

32. Frank B. Jewett, "The Genesis of the National Research Council and Millikan's World War I Work," *Rev. Mod. Phys.* 20 (1948):2.

33. Ira Sprague Bowen, "Astronomical Instrumentation," in Helen Wright et al., *The Legacy of George Ellery Hale* (Cambridge, Mass., 1972), p. 239.

34. "Biographical Notes," Hale Papers, Box 92.

35. G. E. Hale, "The New Astronomy," *Beacon* 1 (1899):164.

36. Hale to Mrs. C. D. Walcott, July 16, 1929, Hale Papers, Box 42.

37. "Biographical Notes," Hale Papers, Box 92, p. 11.

38. Hale, *Astron., & Astrophys.* 11 (1892):17; *Astro. Jour.* 2 (1895):253.

39. Richard Berendzden, "The Origins of the American Astronomical Society," *Physics Today* 27 (1974):32–39.

40. Hale used the term in two ways. The first, and less interesting, involves cooperative collection of data by observation stations. The second involves interdisciplinary research efforts. I shall use the term to refer only to the latter.

41. Hale, "Development of a New Method of Research," *Pop. Sci. Mon.* 65 (1904):5.

42. Noyes to Hale, October 14, 1901; Noyes to Pritchett, November 25, 1901, both in Hale Papers, Box 31.

43. "Biographical Notes," Hale Papers, Box 92.

44. Hale to Mrs. C. D. Walcott, July 16, 1929, Hale Papers, Box 42.

45. Charles D. Walcott to Andrew Carnegie, June 25, 1903, quoted in Howard Miller, "Science and Private Agencies," in *Science and Society,* ed. van Tassel and Hall, p. 219.

46. W. S. Adams, "The Founding of the Mount Wilson Observatory," *Publ. Astr. Soc. Pac.* 66 (1954):267–77.

47. R. L. Waterfield, *A Hundred Years of Astronomy* (London, 1938), pp. 112–13, 278.

48. George Ellery Hale, *Ten Years' Work of a Mountain Observatory* Washington, D.C., 1915), p. 34.

49. W. S. Adams, "George Ellery Hale," *Nat. Acad. Sci. Biog. Mem.* 21 (1941):200.

50. Hale to Walcott, July 24, 1914, Scherer Papers, Box 2, folder 14.

51. Hale to James Scherer, May 9, 1908, Scherer Papers, Box 2, folder 6.

52. Hale to Noyes, December 26, 1908, and January 2, 1909; Noyes to Hale, January 14, 1909, all in Hale Papers, Box 31. Noyes did stay in Pasadena for a short time in 1913 on an unofficial basis.

53. Noyes to Hale, May 2, 1912, Hale Papers, Box 31.

54. R. S. Woodward to Hale, October 15, 1912, Hale Papers, Box 45.

55. Hale to Walcott, July 24, 1914, Scherer Papers, Box 2, folder 5; Woodward to Hale, October 15, 1912, Hale Papers Box 45.

56. Millikan, "Autobiographical Notes," RAM 67.3.

57. Hale to Scherer, March 27, 1913, Scherer Papers, Box 2, folder 5; Noyes to Hale, August 7, 1913, Hale Papers, Box 31.

58. Hale to W. W. Campbell, December 2, 1915, Scherer Papers, Box 2, folder 6.

59. Hale to Scherer, May 30, 1916, Scherer Papers, Box 2, folder 6. Italics mine.

60. Hale to Scherer, July 19, 1916, Scherer Papers, Box 2, folder 16.

61. Hale to Harry Pratt Judson, August 4, 1916, Hale Papers, Box 24.

62. Hale to Scherer, November 1, 1916, Scherer Papers, Box 2, folder 6.

63. Hale to Woodward, January 19, 1917, Hale Papers, Box 45.

64. See Kevles, "George Ellery Hale," pp. 427–37.

65. Hale to Arthur Fleming, March 4, 1918, Hale Papers Box 16.

66. Hale to Evelina Hale, September 1918, Hale Papers, Box 80.

67. Hale to Scherer, November 30, 1919, Scherer, Papers, Box 2, folder 7.

68. Noyes to Hale, November 20, 1919, Hale Papers, Box 32. Right away Noyes began his successful campaign to change the name of the institution from Throop to California Institute of Technology (Noyes to Scherer, December 5, 1919, Scherer Papers, Box 2, folder 19).

69. Hale to Noyes, May 15, 1920, Hale Papers, Box 32; Hale Diary, June 8, 1920, ibid., Box 94.

70. Hale to Millikan, July 4, 1920, RAM 26.4.

71. Millikan to Lewis, March 3, 1920, Gilbert Newton Lewis Papers, University of California, Berkeley.

72. Hale to H. Robinson, February 25, 1921, Hale Papers, Box 35.

73. On May 15, 1921, Hale noted in his diary that with Millikan's coming, Caltech might attract to Pasadena such eminent European scientists as "Majorana, Lorentz, Epstein, Fowler, Fabry, Perrin, Jeans, Eddington, Rutherford, Silberstein, Mees" (Hale Papers, Box 94).

74. Millikan to M. Ryerson February 8, 1921; Judson to Millikan, March 1, 1921, both in RAM 43.11.

75. George Ellery Hale to Evelina Hale, May 18, 1921, Hale Papers, Box 81.

76. Robert A. Millikan to Greta Millikan, May 17, 1921, RAM 50.4.

77. George Ellery Hale to Evelina Hale, May 17, 1921, Hale Papers, Box 81.

78. Judson to Millikan, July 6, 1921, RAM 43.11.

79. Telegram, George Ellery Hale to Evelina Hale, June 1, 1921, Hale Papers, Box 81.

80. Millikan, "Address of Acceptance to the Norman Bridge Laboratory of Physics," *Science* 55 (1922):331.

81. Quoted in N. Reingold, "National Aspirations and Local Purposes," *Trans. Kans. Acad. Sci.* 71 (1968):241–42.

82. National Research Council, *Third Annual Report* (Washington, D.C., 1919), p. 26; Kevles, "George Ellery Hale," p. 435n. Noyes was well acquainted with George Eastman and Pierre Du Pont from his days as acting president of the Massachusetts Institute of Technology.

83. The Woodward folders in RAM 20 contain numerous expressions of praise.

84. Hale to Walcott, January 17, 1920, Hale Papers, Box 21.

85. Quoted in Reingold, "National Aspirations," pp. 241–42.

86. Hale to Charles F. Holder, February, 19, 1912, Hale Papers, Box 21.

87. RAM 59.47.

88. Millikan, "Some Exceptional Opportunities in Southern California," RAM 27.9, pp. 1, 2, 5.

89. Millikan, "The California Institute of Technology: Its Directions,

Aims, Accomplishments, Needs and Financial Condition" (1923), Arthur Fleming Papers, Box 3, folder "Gen. Ed. Bd., "California Institute of Technology.

90. Hale to Pritchett, November 1, 1933, Hale Papers, Box 67, "Carnegie Corporation" folder.

91. Carnegie Institution of Washington, *Yearbook* 18 (1919):226–30, 19 (1920):219–65, 20 (1921):215–42.

92. Ibid., 20 (1921):217–18.

93. Noyes to Leonard Loeb, February 8, 1916, Scherer Papers, Box 2. I am indebted to John Servos for calling my attention to this quotation.

94. Millikan, *Autobiography*, p. 217.

95. George Ellery Hale to Evelina Hale, May 18, 1921, Hale Papers, Box 81.

96. "Plan for an Institute of Physics and Chemistry," Scherer Papers, Box 2.

97. Hale Diary, 1921, Hale Papers, Box 94.

98. Hale to J. Angell, June 4, 1921, Hale Papers, Box 67, "Carnegie Corporation" folder, pp. 1–2.

99. Ibid., p. 2.

100. "Memorandum Relating to the Application of the California Institute of Technology to the Carnegie Corporation of New York for Aid in Support of Project of Research on the Constitution of Matter and the Development of the Scientific Departments of the Institute," Hale Papers, Box 6, "C.I.T." folder, pp. 3, 5, 7.

101. Ibid., pp. 1–2.

102. Millikan, *Autobiography*, pp. 220, 217.

103. Jesse Du Mond, "Paul Sophus Epstein," *Nat. Acad. Sci. Biog. Mem.* 45 (1974):127–52.

104. Millikan to Hale, July 28, 1920, Hale Papers, Box 29.

105. Millikan to Hale, July 16, 1921, Hale Papers, Box 29.

106. *New York Times*, June 12, 1969, p. 47.

107. John G. Kirkwood, O. R. Wulf, and Paul Epstein, "Richard Chace Tolman," *Nat. Acad. Sci. Biog. Mem.* 27 (1952):139–53.

108. Noyes to Scherer, April 27, 1911, Scherer Papers, Box 2.

109. Noyes to Richard Tolman, April 16, 1921, Hale Papers, Box 40.

110. *Bull. Cal. Inst. Tech.* 39 (1930):9–32.

111. Report of the Chairman of the Executive Council, March 10, 1922," Edward Barrett Papers, California Institute of Technology, Box 1, folder 9.

112. Paul Epstein and Paul Ehrenfest, "The Quantum Theory of the Fraunhofer Diffraction," *Proc. Nat. Acad. Sci.* 10 (1924):133–39; Harry Bateman and Paul Ehrenfest, "The Derivation of Electromagnetic Fields from a Basic Wave Formation," *Proc. Nat. Acad. Sci.* 10 (1924):309–74; Richard Tolman and Paul Ehrenfest, "Weak Quantization," *Phys, Rev.* 24 (1924):287–395.

113. Horace Babcock, "Ira Sprague Bowen," Bowen Papers, Box 5, California Institute of Technology.

114. "Graduate Research Activities of the California Institute," December 1926, pp. 4–6, Hale Papers, Box 6.

115. "Research Activities at the California Institute of Technology," October 1928, Hale Papers, Box 6.

116. RAM 25.17.

117. Lawrence Shirley, "Two Decades of Caltech Development," B.S. thesis, California Institute of Technology, 1969, pp. 71–72.

118. The details of von Karman's appointment are ably presented in Paul Hanle's unpublished manuscript "Bringing Aerodynamics to America" (1978), chaps. 2, 6.

119. Wycliffe Rose, head of the General Education Board, had given Millikan great encouragement along these lines in 1923; see Millikan to Hale, August 28, 1923, RAM 26.4.

120. Robert A. Millikan to Glenn Millikan, February 5, 1928, RAM 57.5.

121. On Morgan, see Garland Allen, *Thomas Hunt Morgan* (Princeton, 1978), esp. pp. 334–68.

122. Millikan, "California Institute of Technology," pp. 3–4.

123. Quoted in Reingold, "National Aspirations," pp. 241–42.

124. Herbert Hoover, "The Nation and Science," *Science* 65 (1927): 27–28.

125. Robert Kargon, *The Maturing of American Science* (Washington, D.C., 1974), pp. 22–23.

5. The Scientist as Sage

1. Paul Epstein recalled that "he had too many ideas. I wanted to get people working on some of my ideas, but that was impossible. Millikan had too many of his own, and the men were not available" (*Sources for History of Quantum Physics*, May 26, 1962, p. 7).

2. Dorothy Michelson Livingston, *The Master of Light: A Biography of Albert A. Michelson* (New York, 1973), p. 264.

3. James Mink, "Teacher, Researcher and Administrator: Vern O. Knudsen," UCLA Oral History Project, 1974, pp. 134–35, 143, 127; transcript in Bancroft Library, University of California, Berkeley.

4. A useful review is F. H. Loring, *Atomic Theories* (London, 1921), p. 41–68.

5. Millikan, "Holographic Autobiographical Notes," RAM 67.8.

6. On Moseley's work, see *Phil. Mag.* 26 (1912):1024, 27 (1914):1703. See also John Heilbron, *H. G. J. Moseley: The Life and Letters of an English Physicist, 1887–1915* (Berkeley, 1974), chaps. 5, 6.

7. Moseley, *Phil. Mag.* 27 (1914):703–13. See also Millikan, *The Electron* (Chicago, 1917), pp. 200–202.

8. Millikan, "Radiation and Atomic Structure," *Phys. Rev.* 10 (1917):194–95, 204–5, 225.

9. "Memorandum Relating to the Application of the California Institute of Technology to the Carnegie Corporation for Aid in Support of a Project of Research on the Constitution of Matter," September 17, 1921, in George Ellery Hale Papers, Box 6, p. 1, California Institute of Technology.

10. University of Chicago, *President's Report, 1905–1906*, p. 124.

11. Theodore Lyman, "Spectroscopy of the Ultra Violet," *Astrophys. Jour.* 43 (1916):89.

12. Millikan, *Astrophys. Jour.* 52 (1920):47; Millikan, Sawyer, and Bowen, *Astrophys. Jour.* 53 (1921):150; Paul Epstein, "Robert Andrews Millikan as Physicist and Teacher," *Rev. Mod. Phys.* 20 (1948):19–21.

13. Millikan, *Proc. Nat. Acad. Sci.* 7 (1921):289.

14. Millikan and B. E. Shackelford, *Phys. Rev.* 15 (1920):240.

15. Millikan and Carl Eyring, *Phys. Rev.* 27 (1926):51; Millikan and Charles Lauritsen, *Proc. Nat. Acad. Sci.* 14 (1928):45; *Phys. Rev.* 33 (1929):598; Millikan, Eyring, and S. S. Mackeown, *Phys. Rev.* 31 (1928):900.

16. J. R. Oppenheimer, *Phys. Rev.* 31 (1928):914; R. H. Fowler and Lothar Nordheim, *Proc. Roy. Soc.* 119 (1928):173.

17. C. T. R. Wilson, *Proc. Camb. Phil. Soc.* 11 (1900):52; Julius Elster and Hans Geitel, *Phys. Zeits.* 2 (1900–1901):560.

18. Rutherford and H. L. Cooke, *Phys. Rev.* 16 (1903):183; John McLennan and Eli Burton, *Phys. Rev.* 16 (1903)184.

19. Karl Kurz, *Phys. Zeits.* 10 (1909):834.

20. Karl Bergwitz, *Habilitation-Schriften* (Brunswick, 1910); Albert Gockel, *Phys. Zeits.* 11 (1910):280, 12 (1911):595. I am following the account in Victor Hess, *The Electrical Conductivity of the Atmosphere and Its Causes* (New York, 1938), pp. 115–18, and J. D. Stranathan, *The 'Particles' of Modern Physics* (Philadelphia, 1942), chap. 12.

21. Victor Hess, *Akad. Wiss. Wien Ber.* 120 (1911):1575, 122 (1913):1481; Werner Kolhörster, *Phys. Zeits.* 14 (1913):1066, 1153; *Verh. D. phys. Gesell.* 16 (1914):719.

22. Hess and Kofler, *Akad. Wiss. Wien Ber.* 126 (1917):1389–1436.

23. Millikan to Woodward, May 6, 1919, RAM 20.14. See also Millikan to Henry Crew, March 3, 1920, Crew Papers, Niels Bohr Library, American Institute of Physics, New York.

24. Application to Carnegie Corporation, Hale Papers, Box 6, sec. D, p. 3.

25. Arnold Sommerfeld, *Atombau und Spektrallinien* (Braunschweig, 1922), p. 75.

26. Millikan, *Electron*, pp. 202–3.

27. F. W. Aston, *Isotopes* (London, 1922), p. 90.

28. Ibid. p. 101; W. Harkins and E. Wilson, "Energy Relations Involved in the Formation of Complex Atoms," *Phil. Mag.* 30 (1915):723–34.

29. Aston, *Isotopes,* p. 104.

30. Ernest Rutherford, *Smith. Inst. Ann. Rpt. 1915* (Washington, D.C., 1916), p. 201.

31. Millikan, "Recent Discoveries in Radiation and Their Significance," *Pop. Sci. Mon.* 64 (1904):49.

32. Millikan, "Gulliver's Travels in Science," *Scribner's* 74 (1923): 584.

33. *Nature* 90 (1913):653–54.

34. *Phys. Rev.* 3 (1914):294.

35. Ernest Rutherford, *The Newer Alchemy* (Cambridge, 1937).

36. Millikan to Rutherford, February 3, 1920, RAM 42.

37. Millikan, "The Significance of Radium," *Science* 54 (1921): 59–67.

38. Hale to Henry Robinson, February 25, 1921, Hale Papers, Box 35.

39. Hale to James R. Angell, June 4, 1921, Hale Papers, Box 6.

40. Robert Kargon, "Temple to Science," *Hist. Stud. Phys. Sci.* 8 (1977):1–31.

41. Application to Carnegie Corporation, Hale Papers, Box 6.

42. Caltech Archives, Institute Publicity Releases, Box 31-A, p. 12.

43. Millikan, "Gulliver's Travels," p. 584.

44. He repeated this claim in 1926 ("The Last Fifteen Years in Physics," *Proc. Amer. Phil. Soc.* 65 [1926]:74).

45. Millikan, "Gulliver's Travels," p. 584; italics mine.

46. Royal Sorensen, *Jour. Amer. Inst. Elect. Eng.* 44 (1925):373–74.

47. George Winchester, *Phys. Rev.* 3 (1914):294.

48. *Nature* 114 (1924):197–98; *Naturwissenschaften* 13 (1925):635–37; *Nature* 116 (1925):95–96.

49. *Nature* 117 (1926):13, 621.

50. *Naturwissenschaften* 14 (1926):405–12, *Nature* 116 (1925):902–4.

51. Ernest Rutherford, *BAAS Rpts.* (1923), p. 21.

52. Arthur Eddington, *BAAS Rpts.* (1920), p. 46.

53. Rutherford, *BAAS Rpts.* (1923), p. 21.

54. *CIW Rpts.* 21 (1922):385–86; italics mine.

55. Millikan to Merriam, May 3, 1923, John Campbell Merriam Papers, Library of Congress, Box 125.

56. Millikan, "Atomic Structure and Etherial Radiation," RAM 62.10, pp. 15–16.

57. Marie Curie. *Comptes rendus* 126 (1898):1103.

58. Jean Perrin, *Ann. Physique* 11 (1919):85–87.

59. See, for example, L. R. Maxwell, *Jour. Franklin Inst.* 207 (1929): 619–28; N. Dobronravov, P. Lukirsky, and V. Pavlov, *Nature* 123 (1929): 760; L. N. Bogojavlensky, *Nature* 123 (1929):872.

60. Millikan, *Proc. Nat. Acad. Sci.* 12 (1926):149.

61. Millikan and Bowen, *Phys. Rev.* 22 (1923):198; Russell Otis, *Phys. Rev.* 22 (1923):198–99.

62. Otis and Millikan, *Phys. Rev.* 23 (1924):778–79.

63. Millikan, *Nature* 114 (1924):143; italics mine.

64. Gerhard Hoffmann, *Phys. Zeits.* 26 (1925):669–72; Millikan to Hess, July 24, 1926, RAM 40.9.

65. Millikan, *CIW Rpts.* 23 (1923–24):301.

66. Millikan, *Electrons (+ and –), Protons, Photons, Neutrons, Mesotrons, and Cosmic Rays* (Chicago, 1947), pp. 307–8.

67. Millikan, *Proc. Nat. Acad. Sci.* 12 (1926):53–54.

68. Millikan, *Science and the New Civilization* (New York, 1930), p. 105.

69. Millikan, "The Last Fifteen Years of Physics," *Proc. Amer. Phil. Soc.* 65 (1926):78.

70. *New York Times*, November 12, 1925, p. 24.

71. *Time*, May 23, 1925, pp. 26–27.

72. *Time*, April 25, 1927, cover.

73. Hess, *Phys. Zeits.* 27 (1926):159–64.

74. Millikan to Hess, July 24, 1926, RAM 40.9.

75. Millikan and G. H. Cameron, *Phys. Rev.* 28 (1926):867–68.

76. W. D. MacMillan, "The New Cosmology," *Sci. Amer.* 134 (1926): 310–11; R. A. Millikan, "History of Research in Cosmic Rays," *Nature* 126 (1930):15; R. A. Millikan, Supplement to *Nature* (January 7, 1928):26.

77. Robert A. Millikan to Glenn Millikan, February 27, 1928, RAM 57.5.

78. Millikan, *Pop. Sci. Mon.* 64 (1904):498.

79. Millikan and Cameron, "Direct Evidence of Atom Building," *Science* 62 (1928):401–2.

80. Millikan and Cameron, "The Origin of Cosmic Rays," *Phys. Rev.* 32 (1928):533–57; Paul Dirac, *Proc. Roy. Soc.* 111A (1926):423; Aston, *Proc. Roy. Soc.* 115 (1927):487–514.

81. *Science* 62 (1928):402.

82. Millikan to Glenn Millikan, March 29, 1928, RAM 57.5.

83. *New York Times*, March 18, 1928, p. 1; March 25, 1928, sec. 10, p. 3.

84. Millikan and Bowen, *Proc. Nat. Acad. Sci.* 16 (1930):423.

85. Rutherford, *Proc. Roy. Soc.* 122A (1929):15.

86. Millikan, "The Significance of Cosmic Rays," RAM 63.28.

87. E. C. Stoner, *Proc. Leeds Phil. & Lit. Soc.* 1 (1929):349. See also Stoner, *Phil. Mag.* 7 (1929): 841–58.

88. James Chadwick, *Proc. Roy. Soc.* 132 (1931):343.

89. *Phys. Rev.* 40 (1932):325, 45 (1934):352.

90. Millikan et al., *Phys. Rev.* 61 (1942):397–407; *Nature* 151 (1943): 66.

91. Millikan and Cameron, *Phys. Rev.* 32 (1928):555–57.

92. Millikan, *Nature* 127 (1931):170.

93. Millikan, "What I Believe," *Forum* 82 (1929):197–98.

94. Robert E. Brown to Millikan, May 23, 1922, RAM 32, 37. On Bryan's antievolution crusade, see Paolo Coletta, *William Jennings Bryan* (Lincoln, Neb., 1969), 3:198–239.

95. Brown to Millikan, June 17, 1922, RAM 32.37.

96. Maynard Shipley, *The War on Modern Science* (New York, 1927), pp. 239–41.
97. Norman Furniss, *The Fundamentalist Controversy, 1918–1931* (New Haven, 1954), pp. 70–71.
98. Both drafts are in RAM 32.37.
99. The printed text appears in *Science* 52 (1923):630–31.
100. *Science* 57 (1923):630.
101. Millikan, *Evolution in Science and Religion* (New Haven, 1928), pp. 80–81, 83.
102. Millikan, "What I Believe," p. 193.
103. Millikan, *Evolution in Science and Religion*, p. 88.
104. *Time*, April 25, 1927, pp. 16–17.
105. Nathan Reingold, "The Case of the Disappearing Laboratory," *Amer. Quart.* 29 (1977):81.
106. On Millikan as a public figure, see Daniel Kevles, "Millikan: Spokesman for Science in the Twenties," *Engineering and Science* 32 (April 1969):17–22, and *The Physicists* (New York, 1978), pp. 169–70, 261–63.
107. *Time*, April 25, 1927, p. 16.
108. His popular addresses are collected in RAM 59.1–63.47.
109. Finley to Millikan, August 31, 1934, RAM. 41.30.
110. Frederick Lewis Allen, *Only Yesterday* (New York, 1931), p. 164.
111. Sinclair Lewis, *Babbitt* (New York, 1922/1961), p. 8.
112. Walter Lippmann, *A Preface to Morals* (New York, 1929), p. 240.

6. Recessional

1. Robert A. Millikan to Edward U. Condon, July 30, 1926, RAM 38.14.
2. Millikan to Raymond Birge, January 28, 1929, RAM 38.
3. RAM 38.
4. Ibid.
5. J. D. Stranathan, *The "Particles" of Modern Physics* (Philadelphia, 1942), p. 58. On the constants, see also E. Richard Cohen, Kenneth Crowe, and Jesse W. M. Du Mond, *Fundamental Constants of Physics* (New York, 1957), pp. 112–21.
6. Personal interview with J. A. Bearden, Baltimore, May 16, 1979. A synopsis of Bearden's paper appears in *Phys. Rev.* 33 (1929):1088. See also *Proc. Nat. Acad. Sci.* 15 (1929):528.
7. Raymond Birge, *Rev. Mod. Phys.* 1 (1929):1–73; *Phys. Rev.* 40 (1931):228.
8. Kamekichi Shiba, *Tokyo Inst. Phys. & Chem. Res. Rpts.* 19 (1932):97–121.
9. Ertle Harrington, *Phys. Rev.* 8 (1916):738.
10. Cohen et al., *Fundamental Constants*, p. 116.

11. J. Alvin Bearden, *Phys. Rev.* 48 (1935):385.

12. Robert A Millikan, *The Autobiography of Robert A. Millikan* (New York, 1950), p. 86.

13. J. Robert Oppenheimer and J. F. Carlson, *Phys. Rev.* 39 (1932): 864–65.

14. Oppenheimer to Ernest Orlando Lawrence, January 1932, Lawrence Papers, Bancroft Library, University of California, Berkeley.

15. Arthur H. Compton, *Carnegie Institution of Washington Yearbook* 31 (1931–32):331.

16. Jakob Clay, *Acad. Wetensch. Amst. Proc.* 30 (1927):1115, 31 (1928): 1081.

17. Gerhard Hoffmann, *Phys. Zeits.* 33 (1932):633.

18. Carl Störmer, *Zeits. Astrophys.* 1 (1930):237; G. Lemaitre and M. L. Vallarta, *Phys. Rev.* 43 (1933):87.

19. Compton confided his hunch to J. A. Bearden (interview with Bearden, May 1979).

20. *New York Times*, September 15, 1932, p. 32.

21. *CIW Yrbk.* 31 (1931–32):332.

22. H. Victor Neher to Millikan, November 10 and 20, 1932, RAM 21.18.

23. *New York Times*, December 3, 1932, p. 2.

24. Millikan to Compton, November 30, 1932, RAM 21.18.

25. *CIW Yrbk.* 32 (1932–33):332.

26. Quoted in Daniel Kevles, *The Physicists* (New York, 1978), p. 241.

27. *New York Times*, December 30, 1932, p. 1.

28. Ibid., January 1, 1933, p. 16.

29. Kevles, *Physicists*, p. 242.

30. "Cosmic Row," *Nation* 136 (1933):54.

31. Millikan, Bowen, and Neher, *Phys. Rev.* 46 (1934): 641–52.

32. Ibid., p. 652.

33. *Science* 80 (Suppl.) (October 26, 1934):6–7.

34. Millikan, *Science* 81 (1935):215.

35. Robert A. Millikan, *Electrons (+ and –), Protons, Photons, Neutrons, Mesotrons, and Cosmic Rays* (Cambridge, 1935), p. 410.

36. Ibid., p. 408.

37. Discussion with Clifford Truesdell, April 1976.

38. *Nature* 136 (1935):320.

39. *Rev. Sci. Inst.* 6 (1935):89–90.

40. *Phys. Rev.* 47 (1935):205–8.

41. *Phys. Rev.* 50 (1936):15–24.

42. Compton to Millikan, November 12, 1936, RAM 21.18.

43. Ibid., enclosure.

44. Millikan to Compton, December 4, 1936, RAM 21.18.

45. Compton to John Tate, January 8, 1937, enclosure, copy to Millikan, RAM 21.18.

46. Millikan to Compton, January 19, 1937, RAM 21.18. The copy

in the Millikan collection has written on it: "This letter was not sent to Dr. Compton."

47. Compton to Millikan, August, 23, 1937, RAM 21.18.

48. Clay to Compton, January 3, 1938, Arthur Holly Compton Papers, Washington University, St. Louis.

49. Millikan to Compton, January 19, 1937, RAM 21.18.

50. Campaign address for Hoover, October–November 1932, RAM 59.38.

51. "Science and Social Justice," RAM 60.32.

52. "In the Coming Century" (1934), RAM 60.47.

53. "A Physicist's Dream" (1933), RAM 59.41.

54. "Science Makes Jobs," (1934), RAM 60.1.

55. For the Community Chest (1935), RAM 60.13.

56. "A Physicist's Dream," RAM 59.41.

57. "Excess Government May Spoil the American Dream," RAM 60.4.

58. "Woman's Century" (1937), RAM 60.20.

59. "Science and Social Justice," RAM 60.32.

60. RAM 60.67.

61. RAM 60.68.

62. Daniel Kevles, "The National Science Foundation and the Debate over Postwar Research Policy," *Isis* 68 (1977):11.

63. Quoted in James Penick et al., *The Politics of American Science: 1939 to the Present* (Cambridge, Mass., 1965), p. 314.

64. *Science* 103 (1946):162.

65. Millikan to Frank Jewett, February 28, 1946, RAM 32.38.

66. Millikan to Jewett, March 9, 1946, RAM 32.38.

67. Millikan to Jewett, October 15, 1945, RAM 40.26.

68. Millikan to Jewett, October 21, 1949, RAM 40.26.

69. Ibid.

70. Robert Kargon, *The Maturing of American Science* (Washington, D.C., 1974), pp. 100, 157.

71. For a good assessment of the NSF debate and a discussion of the limitations of the solution, see Kevles, *Physicists*, pp. 349–65, esp. 365–66.

72. *Cleveland News,* May 10, 1950, p. 1.

73. Millikan to L. H. Christie, June 1, 1948, RAM 65.1.

74. Millikan, *Autobiography,* p. 6.

75. Ibid., p. 265.

76. Alfred Kazin, "The Self as History," in *Telling Lives* ed. Marc Pachter (Washington, D.C., 1979), p. 76.

77. See Richard Huber, *The American Idea of Success* (New York, 1971), esp. chap 8; on the self-made man, see Irvin G. Wyllie, *The Self-Made Man in America* (New Brunswick, N.J., 1954), esp. chaps. 2 and 3.

78. Millikan, *The Electron* (Chicago, 1917), p. 5.

79. Millikan, *Autobiography,* p. 278; italics mine.

80. Ibid., pp. 64–66.

81. Ibid., pp. 101–2.
82. Millikan reprints, California Institute of Technology Archives.
83. *Pasadena Star-News,* December 20, 1953, p. 1.
84. Lee Dubridge, *Science* 119 (1954):274.
85. RAM 63.44.

Index

Abbot, C. G., 96, 108
Abel, John Jacob, 118
Adams, Walter S., 108, 156, 165
Advisory, Committee for Aeronautics, 165
Agriculture, U.S. Department of, 116
Allen, Frederick Lewis, 148, 150
American Academy of Arts and Sciences, 78
American Association for the Advancement of Science, 85, 86, 89, 156
American Association of Astronomers and Astrophysicists, 94
American Council of Learned Societies, 12
American Institute of Electrical Engineers, 75
American Philosophical Society, 78, 139
American Physical Society, 17, 66, 78, 124, 152, 153
American Telephone and Telegraph Co., 21, 92
Ames, Joseph S., 152
Anderegg, Frederick, 29, 30
Anderson, Carl, 116, 144, 160
Angell, James R., 87, 105, 110, 111, 131
Anglo-Saxon civilization, 91
Anglo-Saxon race, 77, 98, 104, 106
Annalen der Physik and Chemie, 49
Anthony, William R., 28
Arago, François, 36, 37

"Arian" civilization, 107
Army Ordnance Department, 90
Army Signal Corps, 87
Arrhenius, Svante, 50, 79
Aston, Francis William, 129, 134, 142; Isotopes, 129
Astronomical and Physical Club, 155
Astrophysical Journal, 94, 117
Atomic Energy Commission, 165, 166
Auerbach, Felix, 37
Avery, Elroy, 28; Elementary Physics, 28
Avogadro's number, 151

Babbitt, 148, 150
Bäcklin, Erik, 152
Balboa, 155
Balch, Allan, 118
Barkla, Charles Glover, 124
Bateman, Harry, 109, 115, 116, 118
Bearden, J. Alvin, 152, 153
Becker, J. A., 80
Becquerel, Henri, 39, 42, 51, 52
Begeman, Louis, 62
Bell Laboratories, 120, 163
Bergwitz, Karl, 127
Berkeley. See California, University of, at Berkeley.
Berlin, 67
Berlin, University of, 30, 34, 37, 39, 42, 46
Birge, Raymond, 151, 152
Bjerknes, Vilhelm, 115
Blacker, R. R., 107
Bohr, Niels, 78, 79, 111, 123–26

Bowen, Ira Sprague, 109, 116, 125, 126, 136
Bozorth, Richard, 109
Brackett, Cyrus F., 28
Bragg, W. Lawrence, 123
Bragg, William H., 123
Bridge, Norman, 101, 107
Bridge Laboratory. *See* Norman Bridge Laboratory.
Bridgman, P. W., 76, 78, 87
British Association for the Advancement of Science, 63, 134
Brittain, William, 152
Brown, Robert E., 145, 146
Brownian motion, 63
Bryan, William Jennings, 145, 146
Bryan Bible League, 146
Bryn Mawr School, Baltimore, 47
Bumstead, Henry, 31, 34, 87
Bunsen, Robert, 93
Burton, Eli, 126
Bush, Vannevar, 163, 164
Butler College, 46
Buwalda, John, 117, 118
Byrd, Richard E., 154

Caley, Donald, 157
California, Southern, 105–8, 113, 118, 119, 146
California, University of, at Berkeley, 96, 97, 101, 116, 117, 153
California Institute of Technology, 11, 12, 20, 21, 73, 75, 82, 92, 94, 100–106, 108–11, 114–20, 131–33, 137, 141, 143, 149, 153, 155, 159, 171, 172
Calvinism, 32
Cambridge, University of, 30, 38, 50
Cameron, G. H., 138, 141–43
Campbell, W. W., 99, 146
Canada, 154
Carlson, J. T., 153
Carnegie, Andrew, 95
Carnegie Corporation, 100, 104, 105, 111, 113, 114, 119, 125, 128, 131
Carnegie Institution of Washington, 95–98, 105, 117, 118, 127, 135, 138, 154–56
Carty, John J., 86, 105, 120, 146
Cattell, James M., 85, 119
Cavendish Laboratory, 58, 60
Chadwick, James, 130, 144

Chemical Society (London), 80
Chemical Warfare Service, 89, 90
Chicago, 46, 47, 63, 64, 67, 70, 94, 100
Chicago, University of, 19, 21, 31, 35, 41, 42, 44–49, 54, 58, 59, 78, 82, 89 94, 98–103, 109, 117, 122, 132, 140; Chemistry Department, 54; Pedagogical Department, 117
Christie, L. H., 167
Churchill, Charles H., 28
Civil War, 19, 31, 84, 90
Clark University, 31, 35
Clausius, Rudolph, 39
Clausius-Mossotti formula, 39
Clay, Jakob, 154, 158–61
Clement-Desormes method, 49
Collie, Norman, 130
Colorado River, 107
Columbia University, 28, 30, 33, 34, 36, 42, 46, 84, 99, 100, 118
Committee of One Hundred, 85, 86
Committee on the Coordination of Cosmic Ray Investigations, 156
Compton, Arthur, 21, 80, 142, 144, 152, 154–61
Compton, Karl, 69, 73, 117
Comstock Prize, 78
Condon, Edward U., 151, 159, 163
Conference on Nuclear Physics (London), 157
Congregationalism, 22, 23, 145
Conklin, Edwin G., 145, 146
Cooke, H. L., 126
Coolidge, Calvin, 161
Cornelius, David, 68
Cornell University, 19, 30, 32, 34, 86, 87, 117
Cornu, Auguste, 37
Cosmos Club, 85
Curie, Marie, 51–53, 136, 143
Curie, Pierre, 51, 52
Cushman, Holbrook, 34

Daniels, Josephus, 85
Dartmouth College, 47
Darwin, Charles Galton, 115
Darwinians, 145
Davis, James John, 146
Debye, Peter, 115
Dempster, A. J., 160
Department of Defense, U.S., 166

Deslandres, Henri, 96
Des Moines College, 46
Dewey, John, 47
Dickinson, Roscoe, 109
Dirac, Paul, 142
Dobzhansky, Theodosius, 116
Dodge, Cleveland E., 104
Douglas Aviation Corporation, 107
Drude, Paul, 48, 55, 56; *Theory of Optics*, 48
Duane, William, 79, 80
Dudridge, Lee, 171
Dunn, Gano, 86, 103, 146
Du Pont, Pierre, 104
Durand, W. F., 86

Earhart, Robert, 54
Eastman, George, 104
Eddington, Arthur, 134
Edison, Thomas, 85, 148
Ehrenfest, Paul, 80, 115, 116
Ehrenhaft, Felix, 65
Einstein, Albert, 66, 67, 69–72, 78–80, 116, 142, 143, 145, 148, 171
Eliot, Charles W., 19
Ellis, James, 109
Epstein, Paul, 73, 80, 115, 116
Eyring, Carl, 126

Faraday, Michael, 80
Field Museum, Chicago, 54
Finley, John, 148
Finney, Charles, 23
Fixed Nitrogen Laboratory, 116
Fleming, Arthur, 102, 107
Fleming, Sir John Ambrose, 156
Flexner, Simon, 83, 100, 103, 105, 110
Folwell, William, 19
Forum, 147
Fowler, R. H., 126
Franklin, Benjamin, 73
Fuller, Leonard, 115

Galbraith, John Kenneth, 18
Gale, Henry, 45, 47, 96, 122
Ganot, Adolphe, 28
Gary, Elbert, 104
Gates, C. W., 100, 107
Gates, P. G., 100
Gates Chemical Laboratory, 100, 109, 110, 113, 132

General Education Board, 118
General Electric Co., 20, 86
Geological Survey, U.S., 34
Germany, 38, 41, 50, 67, 85
Getzels, J. W., 77
Gibbs, J. Willard, 31
Gillis, R. C., 107
Gilman, Daniel Coit, 19, 30, 31
Gilmore, Lucien, 115
Gish, Oliver, 158
Gockel, Albert, 127
Göttingen, University of, 39, 42
Goodstein, Judith, 12
Guggenheim, Daniel, 118
Guggenheim Aeronautical Laboratory, 118
Gullstrand, Allvar, 79

Haber, Fritz, 134
Hale, Evelina, 102
Hale, George E., 82–89, 92–115, 119–21, 125, 128, 129, 131, 132, 156
Hall, Edwin H., 31, 33
Hallock, William, 34
Hallwachs, Wilhelm, 56
Harding, Warren G. 161
Harper, William Rainey, 19, 41, 46, 47
Harrington, Ertle, 153
Harvard School, Chicago, 46
Harvard University, 30, 31, 87, 117
Hastings, Charles, 31, 33
Heisenberg, Werner, 78
Helmholtz, Hermann von, 37, 76
Hess, Victor, 127, 140
High Voltage Laboratory, 131, 133
Hill, Archibald Vivian, 118
History of Science Society, 12, 75
Hobbs, George M., 54
Hoffmann, Gerhard, 138, 140
Holder, Charles, 105
Holtz machine, 51
Hooker, John D., 96
Hoover, Herbert, 16, 77, 120, 146, 148, 161, 162; *American Individualism*, 162
Houston, W. V., 153
Hubble, Edwin, 108, 165
Huggins, William, 93
Hughes, A. L., 69
Hull, Gordon, 47
Huntington Library and Museum, 92, 106

Huxley, L. G. H., 159

Illinois, University of, 46, 68, 116

Jackson, P. W., 77
Jena, University of, 37
Jewett, Frank B., 76, 92, 120, 163, 164, 165
Johns Hopkins University, 17, 19, 30–34, 84, 86, 87, 117, 118, 152
Johnson, Thomas, 156
Johonnet, E. S., 47
Judson, Harry P., 100, 102, 103

Kadesch, William, 70
Kalamazoo College, 46
Kapteyn, J. C., 96, 108
Karman, Theodor von, 116
Kaufmann, Walther, 37
Kazin, Alfred, 169
Kellogg, Vernon, 105
Kelly Field, Texas, 136
Kelvin, Lord (William Thomson), 44, 52, 76; *Popular Lectures*, 52
Kennelly, A. E., 89
Kenwood Institute, 46
Kerckhoff, William, 107
Kilgore, Harley, 163, 164
King, Arthur S., 96, 108
Kinsley, Carl, 54
Kirchhoff, Gustav Robert, 37
Klein, Felix, 39
Klein-Nishina formula, 142–44
Knudsen, Vernon, 122, 123
Kofler, M., 127
Kohlrausch, Friedrich, 34
Kolhörster, Werner, 127, 136
Kuhn, Thomas, 77
Kurz, Jacob, 68
Kurz, Karl, 126

Ladenburg, Rudolf, 68
Lake, J. L., 47
Langmuir, Irving, 86
Laue, Max von, 123
Laurence, William, 156
Lauritsen, Charles C., 107
Lawrence, Ernest O., 153
Lebedev, P. N., 115
Lee, J. Y., 63
Lemaitre, G., 154
Lenard, Philipp, 56, 57, 170

Lewis, G. N., 101
Lippmann, Walter, 150
Lindemann, F. A., 138, 140
Little, Arthur D., 16
Lockyer, Norman, 93
London, University of, 118
Lorentz, H. A., 55, 115, 116, 145
Los Angeles, Calif., 106–8
Luce, Henry, 15

Maanen, Adriaan van, 109
McCormmach, Russell, 12
McCoy, Herbert, 54
McLennan, John, 126
MacMillam, W. D., 140–41
McPherson, Aimee Semple, 145–46
Magnuson, Warren, 164
Malthus, Thomas Robert, 16
Manchester, 67
Mann, Charles R., 45, 46, 48
Mann, Thomas, 11
Maquoketa, Ia., 22, 28
Martel, Romeo, 107
Mason, Max, 87, 115, 165
Massachusetts Institute of Technology, 94, 95, 97, 116
Maxwell, James Clerk, 41, 44n
Mees, C. E. K., 86
Mellon, Andrew, 104
Mendenhall, C. E., 86
Merriam, J. C., 86, 105, 117, 135, 146, 156
Merrill, A. A., 118
Merritt, Ernest, 86, 87
Michelson, Albert, 31, 35, 36, 41, 43, 44, 47–49, 54, 59, 64, 66, 76, 96, 101, 108, 115, 122, 169
Michelson-Morley experiment, 35
Miethe, Adolf, 134
Millikan, Allen, 23
Millikan, Daniel F., 169
Millikan, Glenn, 28, 141, 142
Millikan, Grace, 23
Millikan, Greta Blanchard, 48, 52, 68, 83, 86, 103
Millikan, Mabel, 23
Millikan, Marjorie, 23
Millikan, Mary Jane Andrews, 22, 25
Millikan, Max (brother), 23
Millikan, Max (son), 27, 88
Millikan, Silas, 22–24
Mills, Wilbur, 164

Minnesota, University of, 19
Morgan, Thomas Hunt, 116, 118
Morgan Park Academy, Chicago, 46
Moseley, Henry, 123, 124, 128
Mossotti, Ottaviano, 39
Moulton, F. R., 90
Mount Palomar Observatory, 94, 96
Mount Wilson Observatory, 83, 92,
97, 98, 103, 104, 106, 108, 110,
111, 113, 117, 132, 134, 136
Mudd, Seeley, 118
Munich, University of, 34, 115

National Academy of Sciences, 78,
83–86, 99, 100, 105, 129, 139, 163,
164; *Proceedings*, 117, 151, 152
National Broadcasting Company, 162
National Bureau of Standards, 46
National Endowment for the
Humanities, 12
National Research Council, 83, 85–87,
92, 99, 100, 103–5, 109, 110, 120,
146, 162; Research Information
Service, 87
National Research Endowment. *See*
National Research Fund.
National Research Fund, 120, 162
National Science Foundation, 13,
163, 165, 166
National Workmen's Compensation
Bureau, 47
Naval Consulting Board, 85
Neher, H. Victor, 155, 156, 160, 161
Nernst, Walther, 39, 49, 50, 55
Newcomb, Simon, 17, 18
New Deal, 162, 165
New London Experiment Station, 87
Newton, Isaac, 76
Nichols, Edward L., 33
Nichols, E. F., 87, 96
Nichols, H. A., 54
Nobel Prize, 15, 27, 35, 58, 72–74, 79,
80, 99, 103, 123, 148, 152, 154,
157, 160
Nordheim, Lothar, 126
Nordic race, 16
Norman Bridge Laboratory, 101, 103,
113, 132, 134, 159
Northwestern University, 78
Noyes, Arthur, 82, 83, 85–87, 97, 98,
100, 101, 107, 111, 112, 116,
119–21, 125, 128, 132, 146, 156

Oberlin College, 23, 27–30, 41, 42, 49,
78
Office of Scientific Research and
Development, 163
Office of Technological Mobilization,
163
Ohm's Law, 55
Olivet College, 23
Oppenheimer, J. Robert, 116, 126,
153
Osborn, Herbert, 145, 146
Ostwald, Wilhelm, 50
Otis, R., 136, 138

Paris Universal Exposition, 51
Pasadena, Calif., 96, 98–101, 103, 104,
107–9, 116, 118, 119, 123, 135, 146,
171
Patterson, H., 130
Pauli, Wolfgang, 78
Pauling, Linus, 109, 116
Pearson, Julius, 136
Peck, John F., 28, 30, 169
Peltier effect, 55
Perrin, Jean, 136
Philosophical Magazine, 54
Physica, 160
Physical Review, 31, 36, 57, 69, 70, 71
117, 136, 138, 140
Physical Society (German), 39, 67
Physical Society, American. *See*
American Physical Society.
Pickering, E. C., 85
Pierce, G. W., 87
Planck, Max, 37, 67
Pohl, Robert, 69
Poincaré, Henri, 37
Popular Science Monthly, 74, 130, 141
Porter, Noah, 31
Priaulx, D. D., 26
Princeton University, 30, 34, 117
Pringsheim, Peter, 69
Pritchett, Henry, 110
Prout, William, 128, 129
Pupin, Michael, 34, 37, 99, 103, 146,
169

Raman, C. V., 115
Ramsay, William, 53, 130
Regal, Mary, 28
Remsen, Ira, 86
Rensselaer Polytechnic Institute, 33

Rice Institute (Rice University), 87
Richardson, O. W., 69, 70, 73
Riecke, Eduard, 55, 56
Robinson, Henry, 101, 102, 107, 118
Rockefeller, John D., 110
Rockefeller Foundation, 100, 101,
    104, 105, 110, 119
Roe, Edward, 30
Roentgen, Wilhelm, 38, 52, 136
Rood, Ogden, 34–36
Rood, Paul, 146
Roosevelt, Franklin D., 162, 163
Root, Elihu, 91, 104, 105, 111
Rose Polytechnic Institute, 47
Rowland, Henry, 17, 30–34
Royal Society (London), 142, 144
Royal Swedish Academy of Sciences,
    79
Rubens, Heinrich, 37
Rush Medical College, 46
Russell, Henry N., 108
Rutherford, Ernest, 34, 51, 67, 102,
    123, 124, 126, 129, 131, 133, 134,
    142
Ryerson, Martin, 102
Ryerson Laboratory, 35, 42–49, 51, 58,
    63, 66, 83, 132

St. John, Charles, 109
Sawyer, R. A., 125
Scherer, James, 99, 100, 102
School and Society, The (Dewey), 47
Schrödinger, Erwin, 78
Science, 89, 142, 158
Scienservice, 152
Scopes trial, 146
Scribner's Magazine, 132
Seebeck effect, 55
Shackelford, B. E., 126
Shapley, Harlow, 108, 163
Shimer Academy, 46
Small, Albion, 46
Small, Sam, Jr., 132
Smithsonian Institution, 34, 86
Smits, Andreas, 134
Smythe, W. R., 80
Soddy, Frederick, 53
Sommerfeld, Arnold, 111, 115, 128
Sorensen, Royal, 133
Southern California Edison Co., 101,
    102, 107

South Side Academy, Chicago, 46
Squier, George, 87
Stammreich, H., 134
Stanford University, 86, 115
Störmer, Carl, 154
Stokes's Law, 60, 62
Stone, Isabelle, 47
Stoner, E. C., 144
Stratton, Samuel, 45–47, 54
Stuewer, Roger, 72
Sturtevant, A. H., 116
Sunday, Billy, 145
Swann, William F. G., 140
Sweet Briar College, 47

Tait, Peter G., 52; *Properties of
    Matter,* 52
Taft, William H., 77
Terry Lectures, 147
Thackray, Arnold, 12
Thompson, Sylvanus, 30; *Dynamo-
    Electric Machinery,* 30
Thomson, Joseph John, 38, 50, 55–57,
    60, 72, 76, 170; *Discharge of
    Electricity in Gases,* 50, 56
Thomson effect, 55
Throop Polytechnic Institute, 97,
    99–101, 105, 115, 116. *See also*
    California Institute of Technology.
Time magazine, 16, 139, 147, 148
Tolman, Richard, 115, 116
Townsend, J., 72
*Transactions of the New York Academy of
    Sciences,* 36
Trowbridge, John, 31, 33
Troy, University of, 34
Tykosciner, Joseph T., 115

United States Assay Office, 37
University College, 138. *See also*
    London, University of.
Urey, Harold, 163

Vail, Theodore, 104
Vallarta, M. L., 154
Van Hise, Charles, 19
Vassar College, 47
Voigt, Woldemar, 39

Wadsworth, F. L. O., 43
Walcott, Charles D., 95

Warburg, Emil, 37, 79
Watson, E. C., 80, 109
Webster, A. G., 31
Welch, William H., 84, 103, 105, 146
Wellesley College, 47
West, Clarence, 87, 90
Westinghouse Electric Co. 115, 116, 133
White, Andrew D., 19
Whitney, A. W., 47
Whitney, W. T., 109
Wiebe, Robert, 18
Wilson, C. T. R., 60
Wilson, H. A., 60, 61, 62, 72, 87
Wilson, Woodrow, 85
Winchester, George, 55, 57, 130, 132, 133
Winkelmann, Eduard, 37
Wisconsin, University of, 19, 86, 87
Wood, Robert W., 86
Woodward, Robert S., 34, 35, 98, 99, 105, 127

World's Christian Fundamentals Association, 146
World's Work, 18
World War I, 11, 78, 83, 90, 110, 122, 123, 127
World War II, 120, 163
Wright, Frederick E., 156
Würzburg, University of, 34, 38
Wyckoff, Ralph, 109

X rays, 39, 42, 44, 50, 60, 109, 114, 123, 124, 150, 152, 169

Yale University, 30, 31, 34, 87, 117, 147
Yerkes, Robert, 86, 87; *New World of Science*, 87
Yerkes Observatory, 43, 94–96, 98

Zeleny, John, 87
Zwicky, Fritz, 116

The Rise of Robert Millikan

Designed by Richard E. Rosenbaum.
Composed by E. T. Lowe Publishing Co.
in 10 point Linotron 202 Baskerville, 2 points leaded,
with display lines in Baskerville.
Printed offset by BookCrafters, Inc. on
Warren's Number 66 Antique Offset, 50 pound basis.
Bound by BookCrafters in Holliston book cloth
and stamped in Kurz-Hastings foil.

Library of Congress Cataloging in Publication Data

Kargon, Robert Hugh.
  The rise of Robert Millikan

  Bibliography: p.
  Includes index.
  1. Millikan, Robert Andrews, 1868–1953. 2. Physicists— United States—
Biography. I. Title.
QC16.M58K37   530'.092'4   [B]   81-15204
  ISBN 0-9014-1459-8   AACR2